Speedy Weeknight Meals

To Albie. You've made me realise that to grow old is a privilege and this one is for you. You now have twin sisters and I can't wait to show them this when they are older.

• • • • • • •

Speedy Weeknight Meals

JON WATTS

B L O O M S B U R Y   P U B L I S H I N G
LONDON · OXFORD · NEW YORK · NEW DELHI · SYDNEY

Contents

Let's Get Started

For a few years now I've been a bit obsessed with learning what you like to cook and eat at home, through sharing recipes online and analysing your feedback. And I think I've found the answer. You want delicious weeknight meals, put together on a budget, from ingredients you probably have in your cupboard already – or can buy easily in any supermarket – and that can be made in less than 30 minutes. This book is filled with eighty recipes just like that.

I've put them all together here because my goal is to get you cooking. Especially those of you who aren't usually found in the kitchen.

Why? Because, when you ask most chefs where their passion came from, or for their earliest memories of cooking, you will almost always get a similar answer. Often, they have been brought up around food and kitchens and it's in their blood: becoming a chef was their natural next step. For me, that couldn't be further from the truth.

By the time I was eighteen I had never really cooked anything other than a packet of instant noodles, and I hadn't given much thought to cooking either. Food was just fuel. That year – 2008 – I was sentenced to six and a half years in a young offenders' institute. During my time there, I started working in the prison kitchen, originally just to get more food to eat, but the job also came with the highest wage (£12 a week). And yes, you do need money in prison, to buy nicer toothpaste and shower gel, or a duvet: those small comforts that the everyday person takes for granted but which you need to supply for yourself in prison. While I was there, I also started working towards my Duke of Edinburgh awards; I had to pick a skill to learn, and cooking was the obvious choice. During my time in custody – three years and three months in total – I achieved the Bronze, Silver and Gold DofE awards, as well as an NVQ level 3 in professional cookery.

At first this was purely for practical reasons: I wanted qualifications to give me job opportunities once I was released. But while I was learning to cook, I realised I had a natural talent for it, and I liked being praised for it, too. However, my real love for food didn't start until I was leaving prison on day release, working in a restaurant:

that's when I realised that I truly loved it and latched on to that combination of adrenaline and passion of everyone around me in professional kitchens. People often say I am 'lucky' I found my path, but I couldn't see it immediately; instead my way forward became clearer over time. Every day, I find I am more and more passionate about food and cooking, and that continues to grow.

I was released in April 2011, aged twenty-two, with a full-time job in one of Jamie Oliver's restaurants. It was there that a spark was lit inside me... and the fire's still blazing today. I loved the energy-filled environment, the drive of the people I worked with, and finding out about all kinds of new and wonderful ingredients.

Since then, I have gone on to have the most incredible career, which before hadn't seemed remotely possible. I worked in restaurants for several years, before setting up my own business. I started with a food truck cooking on a local high street, as well as at festivals and for private clients. The catering side grew until I was regularly cooking for parties and events all over south east England.

At the start of 2020, I was getting ready to open my own bricks-and-mortar place; it was finally my time to shine. But the universe had other plans: I don't need to remind you what happened next. As restaurants were shut and people were told to stay at home, all my dreams and ambitions vanished overnight and I was left feeling lost.

For the first time in my adult life, I had all the time in the world to think about what to do next. I shared some recipes online and through a local newspaper and I loved knowing that someone I had never met was cooking a dish I had created. Publishing new recipes was always something I wanted to do, but before I had been too busy to get round to it. Now there was no excuse.

The first recipe video I shared on social media was for seared scallops with a truffle and porcini sauce and shaved black truffle. The dish – for two people – probably costs £100 just for the ingredients! No one was ever going to cook it, but they did like to watch someone else make it. Each time I shared a new recipe video, I took note of the analytics to see which were most popular. Naturally, the meals that got more engagement were those that people would cook and eat on a normal weeknight, so fish pie, lasagne and mac n cheese were among the most successful. One day, I was asked by a client to make a chocolate orange cheesecake (you'll find the recipe in this book) and I did and filmed the video, but I worried it wasn't 'cheffy' enough to share online. Working in restaurants, I was used to making fancier puddings. But curiosity got the better of me, so I posted it anyway, just to see how it would do. To my shock, it went viral.

From that moment, I started to try to understand what recipes people wanted to cook. It became like a happy fixation for me and still is. Seeing other people cook my recipes gives me the greatest joy and that is why all the dishes I share are simple, tasty and always use easy-to-find ingredients that don't cost too much.

I wanted to write this book to focus on the recipes that have proved most popular. These are the meals that can be ready quickly – in fact, all of them in less than thirty minutes, apart from the potato dishes in the 'All-Purpose Sides' section – but are packed full of flavour, keeping even midweek dinner times exciting.

I've split the eighty recipes up into seven chapters. There are family favourites for when you have to keep multiple people happy with delicious and nutritious food. There's a chapter devoted to recipes that use six ingredients or less, for when you have limited shopping in the house. We've got quick comfort dishes for those evenings when you need a hug, as well as speedy one-pot meals for no-nonsense food with less clean up. There are fast fakeaway recipes for treat dinners without the expense of a takeaway meal but with all the flavour. I've totted up the numbers for a chapter of low-calorie meals for when you want to keep an eye on what you're eating, and, of course, I couldn't write a book without having a few sweet treats, too.

You will notice there are a lot of chicken recipes here. That's because, if I've learned anything about what you want for your midweek dinner, it's that – for many of you – the answer is chicken! It's quick to cook, familiar, versatile and extremely popular.

Don't worry though, it's not just chicken. The pages that follow are brimming with ideas for all sorts of meals – for vegetarians, pescatarians and red meat fans – and for every occasion from a midweek dinner with friends, to a date night, or just those wet Wednesday evenings when you need to get everyone fed quickly and deliciously without fuss.

Let's get started with speedy meals to give us all more precious time in the evenings, even if we only spend it together on the sofa.

How to cook faster & better

We are all busy, but we still need to eat and *what* we eat is important: a well-balanced diet means we perform better in every other part of life. Good food is also a morale booster: another bonus. When the food coming out of the prison kitchen was better, prisoner morale improved, the level of disruption dropped and you would immediately notice an uptick in general happiness and mood.

All the meals in this book are designed to be speedy and on the dinner table from start to finish in less than thirty minutes. I'm not so naive to think that everyone can cook these meals in the suggested times, as there are so many factors at play, including ability, environment and equipment, not to mention being interrupted by kids, phone calls or life in general. But here are some tips that can help speed up the process.

- Reclaim your kitchen. I see so many kitchens that are used as a storage place. Clear the work surfaces of clutter and put away any big pieces of kit you don't often use.

- The same goes for your cupboards and drawers. Spend some time going through and organising them so the equipment you use the most is easy to find.

- Same goes for ingredients! Are your pantry supplies randomly crammed into any spare gaps? Organise them so you know where they are and so that they're easy to grab.

- Sort out the contents of your fridge and freezer and get to know what's in there. Make a list! This will save you money and prevent food waste, too.

- Invest in the kit you use most: a good knife, chopping board, silicone spatula and frying pan make all the difference.

- Chicken cooks a lot faster than you may think and the timings in my recipes are accurate for my kitchen. If you are at all nervous, either check it with a probe thermometer (which should read 75°C or above), or cut into a large piece of chicken: if you see any trace of pink, cook it for a few minutes more, then test again.

- If you're new to cooking, or lack confidence in the kitchen, then prepare your ingredients before you start a recipe. I find this can make cooking much more fun, too.

- Read a recipe right to the end before you begin, so there aren't any surprises to slow you down.

All-Purpose Sides

How to speed up spuds

This book is packed full of eighty fast weeknight dinners, many of which are super-versatile, so they work well with pasta, rice or potatoes. However, sometimes the type of potato you want to cook takes longer than the main recipe, so here are some tips to speed it up.

- For roasties, pierce whole potatoes with a fork, then pop them in the microwave to par-cook for a few minutes. Continue to peel and roast them as usual.

- Put roasting potatoes on a wire rack placed over the tin, basting frequently with oil, so heat circulates around them more efficiently.

- Use a budget-friendly air fryer, rather than the oven, to almost halve the cooking time.

- Always preheat the oven or air fryer.

- Use a bigger pan than usual, so the potatoes have more space around them and each piece gets more heat.

- Cut them into smaller pieces: quartered baby potatoes are quicker to cook than halved potatoes.

- Mix it up and use sweet potatoes, which cook more quickly than regular potatoes.

Baby hasselbacks   *Pictured on page 152*

● ● ● ● ● ● ● ● ● ● ● ● ● ● ● ● ● ● ●

serves: **4**

1kg baby potatoes
2 tablespoons olive oil
½ teaspoon salt
½ teaspoon black pepper
1 teaspoon smoked paprika
  (not hot smoked)
1 teaspoon dried thyme

1. Preheat the oven or air fryer to 200°C (with the fan on, if you're using an oven).

2. Slice the potatoes two-thirds of the way down, about 2mm apart, and be careful not to slice all the way through. If you place the potatoes between the handles of 2 wooden spoons when you slice them, the handles will stop you cutting all the way through.

3. Tip them into a bowl and scatter over the olive oil, salt, pepper, paprika and thyme relatively evenly. Toss to coat, then tip on to a baking tray big enough so each potato can sit flat on the bottom, with the sliced sides uppermost.

4. Roast for about 45 minutes in the oven, or 30 minutes in the air fryer, until golden and crispy.

Cajun-spiced potato wedges   *Pictured on page 102*

● ● ● ● ● ● ● ● ● ● ● ● ● ● ● ● ● ● ●

serves: **4**

1kg Maris Piper potatoes, cut
  into wedges (no need to peel)
2 tablespoons Cajun spice mix
2 tablespoons olive oil
salt and black pepper

1. Preheat the oven or air fryer to 200°C (with the fan on, if you're using an oven).

2. Pop the potato wedges in a pan of cold salted water. (Starting in cold water helps them to cook evenly.) Bring to the boil, then reduce the heat and simmer for 2 minutes. Drain in a colander and leave to steam dry for a few minutes more.

3. Toss together with the Cajun spice, olive oil, salt and pepper, then spread the potatoes out on a baking tray and roast in the oven for 40 minutes, or air fry for 25–30 minutes, until golden and crisp.

Crispy diced potatoes

Pictured on page 79

• • • • • • • • • • • • • • • • •

serves: **4**

800g Maris Piper potatoes, cut
 into 1cm dice (no need to peel)
2 tablespoons olive oil
1 teaspoon dried thyme
salt and black pepper

1. Preheat the oven or air fryer to 200°C (with the fan on, if you're using an oven).

2. While it's heating up, put the potatoes in a pan of cold salted water. Bring to the boil, then reduce the heat and simmer for 2 minutes. Drain in a colander and leave to steam dry for a few minutes.

3. Toss the potatoes with the olive oil, dried thyme, salt and pepper, then spread them out on a baking tray and roast for 40 minutes, or air fry for 25–30 minutes, until golden and crisp.

Crusted Parmesan potatoes

Pictured on page 37

• • • • • • • • • • • • • • • • •

serves: **4**

750g baby potatoes
60g finely grated Parmesan
 cheese
1 teaspoon garlic granules
1 teaspoon dried oregano
½ teaspoon paprika (not hot)
½ teaspoon black pepper
1 tablespoon vegetable or
 sunflower oil
salt

1. Preheat the oven or air fryer to 200°C (with the fan on, if you're using an oven). Line a large baking tray with baking paper.

2. Cut the baby potatoes in half lengthways, put them into a saucepan of cold salted water and bring to the boil. Reduce the heat to a simmer and cook until they are tender. Drain in a colander and leave to steam dry for a few minutes.

3. Meanwhile, put the Parmesan, garlic granules, oregano, paprika and black pepper in a bowl and mix well.

4. Drizzle the oil into the prepared tray and spread it to the edges to coat the baking paper. Sprinkle over the Parmesan mix evenly so it covers the tray.

5. Place the potatoes on the Parmesan flat side down and press them down firmly.

6. Bake them in the oven for 30–35 minutes, or air fry for 20 minutes. Take them out and leave to rest for 5 minutes.

7. Cut in between each potato so you can remove them individually, then use a flat metal spatula to lift them up and serve.

Potato rosti

Pictured on page 39

• • • • • • • • • • • • • • •

serves: **4**

800g Maris Piper potatoes
1 onion, finely chopped
1 tablespoon plain flour
2 eggs, lightly beaten
½ teaspoon baking powder
leaves from a small bunch of
  sage, finely chopped
1 teaspoon garlic granules
½ teaspoon salt
½ teaspoon black pepper
2 tablespoons vegetable or
  sunflower oil, plus more
  if needed

1. First peel the potatoes, then use a box grater to grate them coarsely.

2. Place the grated potatoes in a clean tea towel and squeeze it tightly over the sink to get rid of the excess liquid, then tip into a large mixing bowl.

3. Add the onion, flour, eggs, baking powder, sage, garlic granules, salt and pepper. Mix well until completely combined.

4. Heat the oil in a large frying pan over a medium heat. Place golf ball-sized pieces of the potato mixture in the hot oil, using the back of a spoon to press them down into discs. You will probably have to cook these in batches, depending on the size of your pan, adding more oil if needed between each batch.

5. Cook for 4–5 minutes on each side until golden brown and crisp. Once cooked, place them on a plate lined with kitchen paper to blot off excess oil.

6. They are now ready to serve. You can also cook them in advance, then reheat them in the oven, if you want.

Simple mashed potato

Pictured on pages 28 and 91

• • • • • • • • • • • • • • •

For extra-smooth mash, use a potato ricer to mash the potatoes before adding the butter and milk.

serves: **4**

1kg potatoes (red-skinned,
  Maris Piper or King Edward)
1 tablespoon salt
100g unsalted butter, plus more
  if needed
100ml milk, warmed, plus more
  if needed
black pepper

1. Peel the potatoes and cut them into quarters. Place them in a deep pot or a saucepan, cover with cold water and add the salt.

2. Bring to the boil over a high heat, then reduce the heat slightly so the water is simmering rapidly. Cook until the potatoes are completely soft and a knife goes through very easily.

3. Drain in a colander, then leave to steam dry for a few minutes.

4. Tip them back into the pot, or into a mixing bowl, add the butter and the warm milk and mash until smooth, adding more milk or butter if you want them. Taste for seasoning and adjust it until you have your perfect mash, then serve.

Spice up your rice

When cooking a speedy weeknight meal, rice is a great choice for a side because it's quick and versatile. It can, however, become slightly samey if you're eating it often. So here are some ways to make it more exciting. Choose just one of these each time you cook rice, to keep life interesting.

- Fry an onion until soft, then toast the rice in the oniony oil, stirring, before adding the cooking liquid.

- Use a well-flavoured chicken or vegetable stock, instead of water.

- Gently cook chopped herb leaves in butter and stir them through the rice before serving.

- Stir in a squeeze of lemon juice, a few knobs of butter, salt and black pepper just before you dish it up.

- Cook the rice in a mixture of half coconut milk and half water, then add finely grated lemon or lime zest at the end.

- Use a pinch of ground spices such as cinnamon, allspice, nutmeg or cloves, fried in butter, then stirred through the rice.

- Add a small amount of turmeric to the cooking liquid, to give a good yellow colour.

- Stir through a splash of soy sauce and a scattering of spring onions and serve alongside Asian-style food.

- Tip cooked, diced crispy bacon, chorizo or pancetta into the pan of cooked rice just before serving.

- Stir through vegetables, such as frozen peas or edamame beans, or briefly stir-fried sliced peppers and mange tout.

Speedy Greens

Roasted sprout gratin *Pictured on page 47*

• • • • • • • • • • • • • • • • •

A spoonful of these creamy sprouts is great alongside Loaded festive turkey schnitzel (see page 46).

serves: **6**

500g Brussels sprouts
2 tablespoons vegetable or
    sunflower oil
30g unsalted butter
30g plain flour
400ml whole milk
1 teaspoon Dijon mustard
75g strong Cheddar cheese,
    grated
150g pancetta lardons
60g fresh breadcrumbs
salt and black pepper

1. Preheat the oven to 180°C fan.

2. Toss the sprouts with the oil and season with salt and pepper. Place them in a roasting tray and roast for 15–20 minutes until they are tender and turning golden brown.

3. Meanwhile, melt the butter in a saucepan over a medium heat, then add the flour and mix to make a paste. Cook for 2 minutes.

4. Gradually pour in the milk, whisking continuously, until you have a smooth sauce. Cook until it has thickened slightly. Add the mustard and the cheese and mix until the cheese has melted, then take the sauce off the heat.

5. Place the pancetta lardons in a cold pan with no oil. Cook over a high heat until they have turned crispy, then use a slotted spoon to take the pancetta out and set aside, keeping the fat in the pan.

6. Fry the breadcrumbs in the pancetta fat; they will start to turn crispy.

7. When the sprouts are nicely golden, toss them with the crispy pancetta and place in an ovenproof dish. Spoon the cheese sauce over, then sprinkle the breadcrumbs on top. Bake for 12–15 minutes, until piping hot and bubbling.

Lemony garlic greens

Pictured on page 167

● ● ● ● ● ● ● ● ● ● ● ● ● ● ●

I always like to add some greens to my meals, so here's a speedy way to make them a little more exciting. You can switch the broccoli for most other greens.

serves: **4**

1 tablespoon vegetable or
  sunflower oil
2 garlic cloves, finely sliced
220g Tenderstem broccoli
75ml water
juice of ½ lemon
1 tablespoon extra virgin olive oil
salt and black pepper

1. Put the vegetable or sunflower oil in a large frying pan over a medium-high heat. Add the garlic and cook for a minute or until it starts to turn brown, but be careful that it doesn't burn, or it will become bitter.

2. Add the broccoli to the pan and pour in the measured water. Cover with a lid or a sheet of foil and cook for 4–5 minutes, or until the broccoli is tender.

3. Season with salt and pepper, then squeeze in the lemon juice, stir through the olive oil and serve.

Honey & thyme roasted roots

Pictured on page 47

● ● ● ● ● ● ● ● ● ● ● ● ● ● ●

The honey here really emphasises the natural sweetness of the carrots and parsnips. Great for winter eating.

serves: **6**

25g unsalted butter
2 tablespoons vegetable or
  sunflower oil
300g carrots
300g parsnips
leaves from 15g thyme,
  chopped
3 tablespoons honey
salt and black pepper

1. Preheat the oven to 180°C fan.

2. Put the butter and oil in a large roasting dish and place it in the oven for 5 minutes to heat up.

3. Meanwhile, cut the ends off the carrots and parsnips, then cut them into thin batons: I cut them in half, then each half into 4 lengthways. There is no need to peel them, just wash them if they are dirty.

4. Add the vegetables and thyme to the dish and turn to coat them in the buttery oil.

5. Roast for 20 minutes, then take them out and add the honey, salt and pepper. Stir them to coat in the honey, then roast for another 20 minutes until crisp and golden.

Family Favourites

If you struggle to find meals that the whole family loves, these are the recipes for you: I've tested them out and I know they are popular with all ages. Some, such as Thai-style chicken satay and Koftes with speedy flatbreads (see pages 22 and 48), are fun to get kids to help with, too. Make them together and use the opportunity to create lasting memories, while craftily promoting healthy eating and encouraging creativity and experimentation with food and cooking.

Thai-style chicken satay

• • • • • • • • • • • • • • • • • •

When I started putting this book together, this was always going to be the number one recipe, which is why it comes first. There's a reason why it's been viewed millions of times online and has been made successfully by so many. Only a handful of ingredients create the most delicious dish in such a short time. I have no doubt you'll make this time and again. It goes well with rice and I like to serve it with sliced cucumber and spring onions, for crunch.

serves: **4**
prep time: **10 mins**
cook time: **15 mins**

300g smooth peanut butter
200g Thai red curry paste
4 tablespoons soy sauce
400ml can of coconut milk
1kg skinless boneless
  chicken thighs
2 tablespoons vegetable or
  sunflower oil
25g coriander, chopped
  (optional)
salt and black pepper

1. Put the peanut butter in a bowl with the curry paste, soy sauce and 50ml of the coconut milk. Beat until smooth.

2. Transfer two-thirds of the peanut butter mixture to a saucepan, add the remaining coconut milk and mix well.

3. Cut the chicken into bite-sized pieces, add it to the bowl of the remaining peanut mix and stir until it's completely coated. Thread the chicken on to 8 skewers that will fit in a large frying pan.

4. Heat the oil in the large frying pan and cook the chicken over a medium heat until golden brown all over and cooked through. (If you cut into a larger piece of chicken, the juices should run clear. If not, continue to cook for another couple of minutes, then test again.) You may need to do this in batches, depending on the size of your pan.

5. Heat up the sauce in the saucepan, taste for seasoning and adjust it if needed, then add the chopped coriander, if you like, and stir well.

6. Plate up the chicken skewers, then either pour over the satay sauce, or serve it in a bowl on the side if you prefer.

Family Favourites

'Marry me' chicken orzo

•••••••••••••••••••••

A fun twist on a favourite. My recipe for 'Marry me' chicken has had millions of hits online, and this lovely orzo creation is inspired by the wonderfully rich flavours of that original.

serves: **4**
prep time: **10 mins**
cook time: **20 mins**

2 tablespoons plain flour
½ teaspoon salt
½ teaspoon black pepper
1 teaspoon paprika (not hot)
400g skinless boneless chicken thighs, cut into bite-sized pieces
1 tablespoon vegetable or sunflower oil, plus more if needed
1 onion, finely chopped
4 garlic cloves, finely chopped
500ml chicken stock
250ml double cream
2 tablespoons sundried tomato paste
2 teaspoons dried oregano
250g orzo
60g finely grated Parmesan cheese
20g basil leaves, torn

1. Mix the flour, salt, pepper and paprika in a bowl, then tip in the chicken. Mix well to coat.

2. Heat the oil in a large frying pan over a medium-high heat. Cook the chicken until golden brown all over, then remove it from the pan, leaving the oil behind.

3. Add the onion to the pan, with a little more oil if needed, and cook until it softens, about 5 minutes. Chuck in the garlic and cook for a further minute before pouring in the stock and cream. Stir in the sundried tomato paste, oregano and orzo.

4. Get the chicken back in the pan and stir it well. Bring to a simmer and cook for about 10 minutes, or until the orzo is cooked and the sauce is creamy. The heat should be gentle: you don't want to boil the orzo.

5. Take it off the heat, stir through the Parmesan and basil, then taste for seasoning, adjusting if needed. If it feels a little loose, leave it to stand for a minute or so, giving the orzo time to soak up the extra liquid, then serve.

Watt's the Story?

It's said that the name of this dish comes from an American workplace in the 1980s, when the recipe for a creamy sundried tomato-infused chicken was being passed around. Three of the women who went on to cook it received proposals soon after. Even if that story is slightly exaggerated, this recipe is so good that you could be at risk of a proposal when you serve it.

Sweet chilli meatballs

• • • • • • • • • • • • • • • • • •

Tasty pork meatballs cooked with a simply great sweet but spiced sauce. Sweet chilli has a universal appeal because it's tangy but not too hot, plus a lot of people will already have it stashed in the kitchen cupboard. This dish goes well with rice and green vegetables, such as pak choi or Lemony garlic greens (see page 19).

serves: **2–3**
prep time: **10 mins**
cook time: **15 mins**

For the meatballs
500g minced pork
1 egg, lightly beaten
40g breadcrumbs
½ bunch of spring onions,
   sliced, plus more to serve
finely grated zest of 3 limes
½ teaspoon salt
½ teaspoon black pepper
1–2 tablespoons vegetable or
   sunflower oil
sesame seeds, to serve

For the sauce
3 garlic cloves, finely chopped
15g root ginger, finely chopped
50ml water
3 tablespoons soy sauce
6 tablespoons sweet chilli sauce
3 tablespoons tomato ketchup

1. Put the pork in a large mixing bowl with the egg, breadcrumbs, spring onions, lime zest, salt and pepper. Get stuck in and mix until it's well combined, then roll it into 12 equal-sized meatballs.

2. Heat the oil in a large frying pan and fry the meatballs over a medium-high heat until golden brown all over. Remove them from the pan, leaving the oil behind, and set aside.

3. Chuck in the garlic and ginger for the sauce and cook them for 30 seconds, then pour in the measured water, soy sauce, sweet chilli sauce and tomato ketchup. Stir well.

4. Get the meatballs back in the pan, turn to coat and bring to a simmer. Cook until the sauce is nice and sticky and the meatballs are cooked through. (If you cut into a meatball, there should be no trace of pink. If there is, continue to cook for another couple of minutes, then test again.)

5. Scatter with spring onions and sesame seeds, then dish them up.

Creamy mustard pork chops

• • • • • • • • • • • • • • •

Who wouldn't be impressed with these? They work perfectly with mashed potato and some seasonal veggies. Go for higher-welfare pork when you can and don't overcook it, but keep it juicy and succulent: that's how to serve pork chops at their best.

serves: **4**
prep time: **5 mins**
cook time: **20 mins**

4 bone-in pork chops, each
   about 2cm thick
2 tablespoons vegetable or
   sunflower oil
25g unsalted butter
1 onion, finely chopped
2 teaspoons dried thyme
2 garlic cloves, finely chopped
180ml white wine, or apple juice
200ml chicken stock, plus more
   (optional) if needed
2 tablespoons wholegrain
   mustard
1 tablespoon Dijon mustard
150ml double cream
20g pack of chives, chopped
salt and black pepper

1. Pat the pork chops dry with kitchen paper, then season generously with salt and pepper.

2. Heat the oil in a large frying pan over a medium-high heat. Add the butter: it should sizzle and melt rapidly. Cook the chops until they are golden brown on both sides, making sure to cook the fat too (if helps to hold them in position with tongs for this), then remove from the pan, leaving the buttery oil behind.

3. Add the onion and thyme to the fat left in the pan and cook until the onion softens.

4. Chuck in the garlic and cook for a further minute before pouring in the wine or juice. Stir well and cook until the liquid has reduced by about half.

5. Pour in the stock, then get the chops back into the pan along with any juices that have come out of them. Cover with a lid or a sheet of foil and simmer for 8–10 minutes, or until the chops are cooked. If the pan gets too dry, just add a splash of stock or water.

6. Add the wholegrain mustard, Dijon mustard and cream and stir well. Taste for seasoning, adjusting it if needed, then sprinkle over the chives and serve.

Pictured with Simple mashed potato, see page 15.

Pesto chicken

• • • • • • • • • • • • • • • • • •

Using a good-quality pesto will transform this dish, plus kids just love pesto, so that makes it easy to feed them. You could substitute cream or crème fraîche for the cream cheese here, but cream cheese is something that families with young children are more likely to already have in the fridge.

serves: **4**
prep time: **5 mins**
cook time: **20 mins**

4 skinless chicken breasts
80g plain flour
½ teaspoon salt
½ teaspoon black pepper
1–2 tablespoons vegetable or
    sunflower oil, plus more
    if needed
1 large onion, finely chopped
250g cherry tomatoes, halved
5 garlic cloves, finely chopped
300ml chicken stock
165g cream cheese (or see
    recipe introduction)
200g basil pesto
25g basil leaves, torn (optional)

1. Cut the chicken breasts in half lengthways to give 8 thinner pieces.

2. Put the flour in a bowl with the salt and pepper and mix well. Dredge the chicken in this seasoned flour.

3. Heat the oil in a large frying pan over a medium-high heat. Cook the chicken until it's golden brown on both sides, then remove it from the pan and set aside, leaving the oil behind. You may need to do this in batches, depending on the size of your pan, as the chicken pieces shouldn't be overcrowded.

4. Add the onion to the pan, with a little more oil if needed, and cook until it starts to soften. Chuck in the cherry tomatoes and garlic, then cook for a further minute. Pour in the chicken stock and bring to the boil, then stir in the cream cheese and add the pesto. Stir well, or leave the pesto in marbled blobs, depending on how you want to present the dish.

5. Get the chicken back into the pan, coat it in the sauce and simmer until cooked through. (If you cut into a larger piece of chicken, the juices should run clear. If not, continue to cook for another couple of minutes, then test again.) When it is cooked, the sauce should have thickened up nicely.

6. Taste for seasoning, adjust it if you want to, then sprinkle in the torn basil leaves, if you want, and serve.

Hot honeyed chicken stir-fry

· · · · · · · · · · · · · · · · ·

You may well have most of the ingredients to make this in the cupboard already. It's hot, spicy and tasty, but if you want to reduce the heat level, just use less sriracha. Serve with basmati or jasmine rice.

serves: **4**
prep time: **10 mins**
cook time: **15 mins**

800g skinless boneless
   chicken thighs
3 tablespoons cornflour
1–2 tablespoons vegetable or
   sunflower oil
1 red pepper, sliced
5–6 spring onions, sliced into
   2.5cm pieces
4 garlic cloves, finely chopped
15g root ginger, finely chopped
6 tablespoons soy sauce
4 tablespoons sriracha
4 tablespoons honey
3 tablespoons tomato ketchup
juice of 2 limes

To serve (optional)
sesame seeds
sliced spring onions
finely sliced red chillies

1. Cut the chicken into bite-sized pieces. Pop them into a bowl, then add the cornflour and stir to coat.

2. Heat the oil in a large frying pan over a medium-high heat. Cook the chicken until it's golden and crispy all over. Add the red pepper and spring onions and stir-fry for a couple of minutes.

3. Chuck in the garlic and ginger and cook for a further minute.

4. Pour in the soy sauce, sriracha, honey, ketchup and lime juice. Bring to the boil, then cook until the sauce is bubbling and sticky and the chicken is cooked through. (If you want to check, slice into the thickest part of the chicken: you should see no trace of pink. If you do, cook for a few minutes more, then test again.)

5. Dish it up, sprinkling over some sesame seeds, spring onions and red chillies, if you like.

Bacon & greens pasta

• • • • • • • • • • • • • • • •

Put this pasta salad on the table, with its crispy bacon and veggies in a creamy sauce, add garlic bread on the side if you like, and the family will be asking for seconds in no time. When getting kids to eat more greens, my secret is to throw in bacon!

serves: **4**
prep time: **5 mins**
cook time: **15 mins**

300g pasta shapes (we used fusilli for the photo)
200g frozen green beans
1 tablespoon vegetable or sunflower oil
250g bacon lardons
1 onion, finely chopped
2 garlic cloves, finely chopped
80g baby spinach
5–6 spring onions, sliced
100ml crème fraîche
100g mayonnaise
finely grated zest and juice of 1 lemon
salt

1. Cook the pasta in salted boiling water according to the packet instructions. Add the green beans for the last 3 minutes, then drain.

2. Meanwhile, heat the oil in a large frying pan and cook the bacon lardons until crisp and golden. Add the onion and cook for 5 minutes more, or until it softens. Now chuck in the garlic and cook for a further minute.

3. Take the pan off the heat, then add the drained pasta and green beans, the baby spinach, spring onions, crème fraîche, mayonnaise, lemon zest and juice and stir well until it's combined.

4. Taste for seasoning, adjusting it if needed, then serve the pasta on a warmed serving dish.

Creamy mushroom chicken

• • • • • • • • • • • • • • • • • •

This combines tender chicken breast and a garlicky mushroom sauce and it has had millions of views online. It's a classic Jon Watts recipe: straightforward and does what it says on the tin.

serves: **2–3**
prep time: **10 mins**
cook time: **15 mins**

2 skinless chicken breasts
60g plain flour
1 teaspoon salt
1 teaspoon black pepper
1 tablespoon vegetable or
    sunflower oil
25g unsalted butter
250g mushrooms, sliced
4 garlic cloves, finely chopped
1 teaspoon dried thyme
200ml chicken stock
150ml double cream
1 teaspoon Dijon mustard
10g parsley leaves, chopped

1. Slice the chicken breasts in half lengthways to give 4 thinner fillets.

2. Tip the flour into a dish or on to a plate, add the salt and pepper and mix well. Coat the chicken in this seasoned flour.

3. Heat the oil in a large frying pan over a medium-high heat, then cook the chicken for a few minutes, turning, until it's golden on both sides. Remove the chicken from the pan, then add the butter. When the butter melts, add the sliced mushrooms and cook for about 5 minutes until they turn nice and golden.

4. Chuck in the garlic and thyme and cook for a further minute before pouring in the stock and cream and adding the mustard.

5. Stir well, then get the chicken back into the pan. Cook until the sauce thickens and the chicken is cooked through. (If you cut into a larger piece of chicken, the juices should run clear. If not, continue to cook for another couple of minutes, then test again.)

6. Add the parsley, stir it through, then season to taste and enjoy with potatoes, pasta or rice.

Pictured with Crusted Parmesan potatoes, see page 14.

Caprese chicken

• • • • • • • • • • • • • • • • •

This Italian-inspired dish is so delicious. It's also a way of sneaking in some more veggies, with the spinach and the tomatoes mixed into the creamy sauce. I love that the red tomatoes, green spinach and white cream all make up the colours of the Italian flag, too.

serves: **2**
prep time: **5 mins**
cook time: **15 mins**

2 skinless chicken breasts
50g plain flour
2 tablespoons vegetable or
  sunflower oil
1 onion, finely chopped
150g cherry tomatoes, halved
4 garlic cloves, finely chopped
150ml chicken stock
150ml double cream
80g baby spinach
50g finely grated Parmesan
  cheese, plus more (optional)
  to serve
salt and black pepper

1. Slice the chicken breasts in half lengthways to give 4 thinner pieces.

2. Tip the flour into a bowl, then season it with salt and pepper. Coat the chicken in the seasoned flour.

3. Heat 1 tablespoon of the oil in a large frying pan over a medium-high heat. Cook the chicken until golden brown on both sides, then remove it from the pan.

4. Add the remaining 1 tablespoon of oil to the same pan, then fry the onion for 4–5 minutes, stirring occasionally until it softens. Add the cherry tomatoes and cook for a few more minutes, until they start to blister. Chuck in the garlic and cook for a further minute. Pour in the stock and cream, then add the spinach. Cook until the spinach has wilted into the creamy tomato sauce.

5. Get the chicken back into the pan, then simmer until the sauce thickens slightly and the chicken is cooked through (3–4 minutes). Add the grated Parmesan and stir well.

6. Taste for seasoning and adjust that if needed, then dish it up with more Parmesan, if you like.

Pictured with Potato rosti, see page 15.

Spicy pork peanut noodles

These great Thai-style noodles use minced pork, making the dish a bit more budget-friendly. Crunchy peanut butter is fine to use here, if that's what you have in the cupboard, but take care the crunchy bits don't stick to the pan and burn.

serves: **4**
prep time: **5 mins**
cook time: **10 mins**

1 tablespoon vegetable or
   sunflower oil
500g minced pork
2 garlic cloves, finely chopped
3 tablespoons Thai red
   curry paste
400ml can of coconut milk
200ml chicken stock
2 tablespoons soy sauce
120g peanut butter, ideally smooth
   (or see recipe introduction)
550g ready-cooked egg
   noodles
juice of 2 limes
80g baby spinach
15g coriander, or parsley
   leaves, chopped

To serve (optional)
chopped peanuts
sriracha
lime wedges

1. Heat the oil in a large frying pan over a high heat. Add the minced pork, then use a wooden spoon or spatula to break it up and cook, stirring and breaking it up, until it's browned all over.

2. Reduce the heat to medium-high. Add the garlic and curry paste and cook for 2 more minutes, stirring occasionally. Pour in the coconut milk, stock and soy sauce, stir well and bring to a simmer.

3. Add the peanut butter, mix well and cook for a couple more minutes. If it gets too dry, just add a splash of water.

4. Toss through the noodles, lime juice and baby spinach. Cook until it's all warmed through, then stir in the herbs and serve immediately, scattered with chopped peanuts, a drizzle of sriracha and lime wedges, if you like.

Cajun chicken pasta

• • • • • • • • • • • • • • • • • • •

Where Italy meets Louisiana! Cajun seasoning is a blend of spices from America's Deep South that creates a spicy, earthy and smoky flavour, and, when combined with a creamy chicken pasta, makes a lovely meal. This dish has been super-popular online, so have a go and see what all the fuss is about: Cajun flavours really go down well with loads of people, it seems.

serves: **2–3**
prep time: **5 mins**
cook time: **15 mins**

200g pasta shapes (we used rigatoni for the photo)
2 skinless chicken breasts
3 tablespoons Cajun spice mix
2 tablespoons vegetable or sunflower oil
20g unsalted butter
4 garlic cloves, finely chopped
1 tablespoon tomato purée
150ml chicken stock
200ml double cream
80g finely grated Parmesan cheese, plus more to serve
15g parsley leaves, chopped
salt and black pepper

1. Cook the pasta in salted boiling water for 2 minutes less than the packet states.

2. Meanwhile, cut the chicken into bite-sized pieces, pop it into a bowl and add 2 tablespoons of the Cajun spice and 1 tablespoon of oil. Stir to coat.

3. Put the butter and remaining oil into a large frying pan set over a medium-high heat. Once the butter melts, add the chicken and cook for a few minutes until it's browned all over. Add the garlic and cook for a minute more, then add the tomato purée and remaining 1 tablespoon of Cajun spice and stir well. Pour in the stock and cream, then bring to the boil and simmer until the sauce thickens up well.

4. Drain the pasta, but reserve some of the cooking water. Add the drained pasta to the sauce and stir well. If it needs loosening up, add a ladle of the reserved pasta water.

5. Stir in the grated Parmesan, then season to taste.

6. Sprinkle in the parsley and stir it through, then grate over some more Parmesan to serve.

Pea & pancetta risotto

• • • • • • • • • • • • • • • • • •

One of my go-to dishes for when I want to impress someone without any faff. I have often cooked this as a dinner party starter and it's always a crowd-pleaser. Serve it with focaccia or garlic bread and a rocket salad.

   If you prepare the risotto base in advance – up to the point when the rice is cooked and you've added all the stock, but before the Parmesan goes in – it'll keep in the fridge for two days, or freeze for up to a month.

serves: **4**
prep time: **10 mins**
cook time: **20 mins**

1 litre chicken stock
1 tablespoon olive oil
1 onion, finely chopped
250g pancetta lardons
300g risotto rice
4 garlic cloves, finely chopped
1 red chilli, finely chopped
  (optional)
100g finely grated Parmesan
  cheese, plus more to serve
80g unsalted butter, diced
150g frozen peas
15g parsley leaves, chopped
salt and black pepper

1. Pour the stock into a saucepan set over a medium-high heat and leave to simmer.

2. Heat the oil in a large frying pan over a medium-high heat. Fry the onion and pancetta until the onion softens and the pancetta starts to turn crispy, then tip in the rice. It's important to toast the rice before adding any liquid, as this enables it to soak up all the flavours. When the rice starts to crackle and pop, add the garlic and chilli, if using, and cook for a minute, until aromatic. Now start to ladle in the hot stock, stirring the rice between each addition.

3. Keep adding the stock bit by bit, stirring continuously and allowing the rice to absorb the liquid each time, until the rice is al dente, then turn off the heat.

4. When the rice is fully cooked, add the Parmesan, butter, peas and parsley, then stir until the cheese and butter melts. Taste for seasoning then serve immediately, with more Parmesan on the side.

Watt's the Story?

Stirring the rice releases its starch and helps to create a risotto's distinct creamy texture.

Loaded festive turkey schnitzel

• • • • • • • • • • • • • • • • • •

Ideal for a celebration lunch, this is ready so fast that you can get back to the Christmas telly or your new presents in no time... Try it with my Crispy diced potatoes (see page 14), roast carrots and parsnips and sprout gratin, add cranberry sauce and/or bread sauce and enjoy! All year round, you can make this recipe with chicken, too.

serves: **4**
prep time: **15 mins**
cook time: **15 mins**

600g skinless turkey breast, cut
   into 4 equal portions
80g unsalted butter, softened
8 tablespoons cranberry sauce
140g Brie cheese, sliced
8 slices of prosciutto
80g plain flour
2 eggs, lightly beaten
250g breadcrumbs
vegetable or sunflower oil,
   to shallow-fry

1. Fold a long length of clingfilm over itself to create a sheet of multiple layers. Place each portion of turkey breast on to a sheet of baking paper, then place the clingfilm over the top. Bash with a meat tenderiser or a rolling pin until the turkey has flattened into a thin escalope, about 5mm thick, being careful not to break the meat. Repeat to flatten all 4 pieces.

2. Mix the softened butter with the cranberry sauce until it's well combined. Divide the cranberry butter between the 4 escalopes and spread it over, leaving a 5mm border around the edges. Lay the Brie over the butter generously, then lay the slices of prosciutto over the cheese to cover.

3. Use the clingfilm again to cover each escalope in turn, then bash lightly to seal the prosciutto over the top.

4. Place the flour in one dish, the beaten eggs in another and the breadcrumbs in a third. Coat each escalope in the flour, then in the egg, and finally in the breadcrumbs. Be careful that you cover each of them all over.

5. Heat a good amount of oil in a large frying pan over a medium-high heat: you need enough oil to come halfway up the sides of the schnitzels. Shallow-fry them for 3–4 minutes on each side, or until cooked through and golden brown. (If you cut into a thick piece of turkey, the juices should run clear. If not, continue to cook for another couple of minutes, then test again.) You will probably have to do this in batches, unless you have a very big pan. Place on a plate lined with kitchen paper, to blot off excess oil, then serve.

Pictured with Roasted sprout gratin and Honey & thyme roasted roots, see pages 18 and 19.

Family Favourites

Koftes with speedy flatbreads

My take on a popular Middle Eastern street food. These are juicy and full of intense flavour that will take your tastebuds on a culinary adventure. I'm sharing the recipes for the flatbreads, tzatziki and crunchy salad too, but if you want to make this even speedier you can buy those from the shop.

serves: **4**
prep time: **15 mins**
cook time: **15 mins**

For the koftes
500g minced lamb
250g minced beef
1 tablespoon dried mint
1 tablespoon paprika (not hot)
1 tablespoon ground cumin
1 tablespoon garlic power
½ teaspoon ground cinnamon
salt and black pepper

For the flatbreads
300g self-raising flour
1 teaspoon baking powder
1 teaspoon cumin seeds
200g Greek or natural yogurt
3 tablespoons vegetable oil

For the tzatziki
½ cucumber
250g Greek yogurt
1 garlic clove, finely chopped
10g mint leaves, chopped
finely grated zest of ½ lemon
  and the juice of 1

For the crunchy salad
150g red cabbage, finely sliced
100g sugar snap peas, halved
1 large carrot, grated
15g mint leaves, chopped
2 tablespoons olive oil

1. Preheat the oven to 200°C fan.

2. Pop all the kofte ingredients into a mixing bowl with ½ teaspoon each of salt and black pepper, then get stuck in with your hands and mix until they are well combined. Divide the mixture into 8, then shape each portion on to metal or wooden skewers. (Alternatively, you can shape them into small burgers, or sausage shapes.)

3. Place them on a baking tray and cook in the oven for 12–15 minutes, or until cooked. (If you cut into a kofte, there should be no trace of pink. If there is, continue to cook for another couple of minutes, then test again.)

4. Meanwhile, for the flatbreads, put all the ingredients except the oil in a mixing bowl and mix. When it starts to make a dough, press it together with your hands.

5. Divide the dough into 8 balls, dust a work surface with flour, then roll each out to about 2mm thick.

6. Place a large frying pan or griddle pan over a medium-high heat. Once hot, add 1 teaspoon of oil. Cook a flatbread for 1–2 minutes on each side until it puffs up. Repeat to cook all the flatbreads, wrapping them in a clean tea towel to keep them warm and soft.

7. For the tzatziki, cut the cucumber in half lengthways, then use a teaspoon to scrape out the seeds. (This stops the tzatziki from being too runny.) Finely chop it, then mix all the ingredients together, using only half the lemon juice. For the crunchy salad, mix all the ingredients together with the remaining lemon juice. Serve the kofte with the flatbreads, tzatziki and crunchy salad.

Chicken with bacon & garlic

• • • • • • • • • • • • • • • • • • •

Tender chicken breasts in a simple sauce with bacon: you can't go wrong. It combines most people's favourite ingredients – cream, chicken and bacon – to create a really tasty dish. Nothing fancy, but most certainly tasty.

serves: **4**
prep time: **5 mins**
cook time: **15 mins**

80g plain flour
½ teaspoon salt
½ teaspoon black pepper
1 teaspoon paprika (not hot)
4 skinless chicken breasts
40g unsalted butter
2 tablespoons vegetable or
   sunflower oil
250g bacon lardons, or
   chopped bacon rashers
1 large onion, finely chopped
5 garlic cloves, finely chopped
800ml chicken stock
240g cream cheese
2 teaspoons Dijon mustard
25g parsley leaves, chopped

1. Put the flour, salt, pepper and paprika into a dish and stir to mix.

2. Cut the chicken breasts in half lengthways to give 8 thinner pieces, then coat each piece in the seasoned flour.

3. Put the butter and oil into a large frying pan over a medium-high heat. Cook the chicken pieces until they are golden brown on both sides. Once cooked, remove them from the pan, leaving the buttery juices behind. (If you cut into a larger piece of chicken, the juices should run clear. If not, continue to cook for another couple of minutes, then test again.) You may need to do this in batches, depending on the size of your pan.

4. Add the bacon to the pan and cook until it starts to turn crispy, then add the onion and cook for a few more minutes until it starts to soften. Add the garlic and cook for another minute, before pouring in the stock. Get the chicken back into the pan and cook until it warms through.

5. Stir through the cream cheese, mustard and parsley until it's well combined, then dish it up.

There's a lot you can make with just a little. The recipes in this chapter all use less than six ingredients – not counting oil, water or salt and pepper – to create easy meals that are truly delicious. You may well have a couple of these ingredients in already, making the dishes even more effortless and kinder on the pocket, too.

Six Ingredients or Less

Red pepper & feta pasta

A super-simple meat-free pasta that's packed full of flavour, and the blender does all the work to create the sauce. Dish it up with the peppery rocket and maybe even some garlic bread. Social media has opened up the world to unconventional and wonderful recipe creations and people are not afraid to try combinations of flavours that aren't traditional. I love that there are fewer norms these days: you can combine feta or Cajun spices with pasta (I've done both in this book) and they will work together.

serves: **2**
prep time: **5 mins**
cook time: **15 mins**

200g pasta shapes (we used farfalle for the photo)
460g jar of roasted red peppers, drained
200g feta cheese
2 garlic cloves
40g rocket

From the storecupboard
salt and black pepper

1. Cook the pasta in salted boiling water for 2 minutes less than the packet states. Drain, but reserve some of the cooking water.

2. Meanwhile, blend the drained roasted red peppers, most of the feta (keep some to crumble on top) and all the garlic until smooth. Pour the sauce into a pan and warm it gently over a medium heat.

3. Add the drained pasta to the sauce, along with a little of the reserved cooking water to loosen it up. Stir until the sauce coats the pasta nicely.

4. Stir through half the rocket until it wilts slightly, then taste for seasoning and adjust if needed. (You shouldn't need to add salt, because of the feta.)

5. Serve, crumbling over the remaining feta and scattering with the rest of the rocket.

Gnocchi cacio e pepe

· · · · · · · · · · · · · · · ·

Cacio e pepe translates to 'cheese and pepper' and that is exactly what this irresistible dish is. Traditionally, pecorino is used, a hard sheep's milk cheese similar to Parmesan which is easy to find in UK supermarkets. This is perfect when you want a great Italian-inspired meal in 15 minutes.

serves: **2**
prep time: **5 mins**
cook time: **10 mins**

400g gnocchi
40g unsalted butter
40g finely grated pecorino
  cheese, plus more (optional)
  to serve
10g parsley leaves, chopped

From the storecupboard
salt
1 teaspoon coarsely ground
  black pepper

1. Cook the gnocchi in plenty of salted boiling water, according to the packet instructions. Drain, but reserve some of the cooking water.

2. Meanwhile, melt the butter in a frying pan over a medium heat. Once it starts foaming, add the black pepper and cook for a minute, until fragrant.

3. Add about 40ml of the gnocchi cooking water to the pan and stir until the sauce has emulsified.

4. Add the drained gnocchi to the pan along with the grated pecorino. Toss until the cheese has melted and you have a smooth, glossy sauce. If it needs loosening up, add a little more of the reserved cooking water. Sprinkle in the chopped parsley and stir well.

5. Divide between 2 warmed bowls and finish with more grated cheese, if you like.

Pasta alla norma

• • • • • • • • • • • • • • • •

A meal inspired by the flavours of Sicily. *It is* said to have been named for the cry of joy and approval that Sicilians could not contain after they tasted this dish, as *norma* means 'masterpiece'. I would heartily agree, as I think aubergine is one of the most underrated vegetables.

serves: **2**
prep time: **15 mins**
cook time: **15 mins**

1 aubergine
4 garlic cloves, finely sliced
400g can of chopped
   tomatoes
200g spaghetti
20g basil leaves, torn
20g Parmesan cheese, to serve

From the storecupboard
olive oil
salt

1. Cut the aubergine into 2cm cubes, pop them into a colander, then sprinkle over some salt. Leave to stand over a bowl or the sink for 10 minutes to extract any moisture.

2. Heat 1 tablespoon of oil in a pan over a medium-high heat, add the garlic and cook for a minute, before tipping in the tomatoes. Rinse out the can with a little bit of water and add that, too. Bring to the boil, then reduce the heat and simmer for a few minutes.

3. Meanwhile, cook the pasta in salted boiling water for 2 minutes less than the packet states.

4. At the same time, pat the aubergine dry with kitchen paper, then heat a good amount of oil - enough to lie about 2mm deep - in a frying pan. Shallow-fry the aubergine over a high heat until it's golden brown, then remove it from the pan and pop on to a plate lined with kitchen paper to get rid of any excess oil. Add it to the tomato sauce and stir well.

5. Drain the pasta, but keep some of the cooking water. Add the drained pasta to the sauce and stir well to coat it. If the sauce needs loosening up a bit, add some of the reserved cooking water.

6. Stir through the basil leaves, then taste for seasoning, adjusting it if needed. Serve the pasta with grated or shaved Parmesan.

Watt's the Story?

The aubergines here are salted, which draws moisture out of their flesh and means they absorb less oil when you cook them. The salting process also removes any bitterness, though these days aubergines are unlikely to taste very bitter.

Salmon, asparagus & pea pilau

• • • • • • • • • • • • • • • •

Create a new weeknight favourite with this healthy rice dish filled with chunky flaked salmon. It's a good recipe to double up, then pop in a tub in the fridge and eat for lunch over the next couple of days.

serves: **2**
prep time: **5 mins**
cook time: **20 mins**

2 skinless salmon fillets
1 onion, finely chopped
150g basmati rice
½ teaspoon ground turmeric
100g asparagus spears,
  halved lengthways
100g frozen peas

From the storecupboard
1 tablespoon vegetable or
  sunflower oil, plus more
  if needed
salt and black pepper

1. Heat the oil in a large frying pan over a medium-high heat. Season the salmon with salt and pepper, then cook it for 3–4 minutes on each side or until cooked through. Remove it from the pan and set aside, covered with foil to keep warm.

2. Add the onion to the same pan, with a splash more oil if needed, and cook until it softens.

3. Tip in the rice, stir to coat, then cook for a minute, stirring often.

4. Pour in 300ml water, season with salt and add the turmeric. Bring it to the boil, then reduce the heat to a simmer and cook for 5 minutes.

5. Stir in the asparagus and peas, then carry on cooking until the liquid has been absorbed.

6. Take the pan off the heat, then leave it to stand for a minute before fluffing it up with a fork. Taste for seasoning, adjusting it if needed, then flake over the cooked salmon in large pieces to serve.

Watt's the Story?

Vegetables in season – such as UK-grown asparagus in spring – are both cheaper and better tasting than imported veg. If asparagus isn't in season when you want to make this, Tenderstem broccoli spears make a good substitute. Frozen veg, such as peas, are great quality and value all year round.

Meatball carbonara

• • • • • • • • • • • • • • • •

A fun twist on a classic, turning sausagemeat into meatballs. Just don't tell your Italian friends what you're doing!

serves: **2**
prep time: **15 mins**
cook time: **15 mins**

200g penne, or any other
   pasta shapes you have
80g finely grated Parmesan
   cheese
1 egg, plus 2 egg yolks
4 sausages, ideally higher-
   welfare and well-seasoned
½ onion, finely chopped
10g parsley leaves, chopped

From the storecupboard
1–2 tablespoons olive oil
salt and black pepper

1. Cook the pasta in salted boiling water for 2 minutes less than the packet states. Drain, but reserve some of the pasta water.

2. Meanwhile, in a small bowl, combine the Parmesan, whole egg and egg yolks. Add a pinch of black pepper, then use a fork to beat it together to form a paste.

3. Squeeze the sausagemeat from the skins, then roll the meat into small meatballs.

4. In a large frying pan, cook the sausage meatballs and onion in the oil over a medium-high heat for about 5 minutes, or until the onion softens and the meatballs start to brown. Add a ladle of pasta water and turn off the heat.

5. Add the drained pasta to the pan and toss it through the meatballs and onion, then add the cheese and egg mixture. Stir well with a pair of tongs to create a creamy sauce. If it needs loosening up, splash in some more pasta water. If it needs thickening up, then cook over a gentle heat while stirring, but be careful not to let the eggs scramble.

6. Stir through the parsley, taste for seasoning and adjust that if needed, then serve it straight away in warmed dishes or plates.

Cajun-spiced cod

A flavourful and delicious dinner where the oven does all the work for you. The juices from the cod and the butter fall on to the broccoli, creating a flavour explosion.

serves: **2**
prep time: **10 mins**
cook time: **15 mins**

200g Tenderstem broccoli
2 × 150g skinless cod fillets
100g unsalted butter, melted
4 garlic cloves, finely chopped
2½ tablespoons Cajun
  spice mix
120g basmati rice

From the storecupboard
salt and black pepper

1. Preheat the oven to 200°C fan.

2. Lay the broccoli in a large baking dish and place the cod on top. Season with salt and pepper.

3. Put the melted butter in a small bowl along with the garlic and 2 tablespoons of the Cajun spice and mix it well. Spread it evenly over the fish, letting it drizzle into the broccoli too.

4. Bake for 15 minutes, or until the fish is cooked: the flesh should begin to flake apart when gently pressed with a fork.

5. Meanwhile, cook the rice according to the packet instructions, adding the remaining ½ tablespoon of Cajun spice to the cooking water. Serve the rice with the cod and broccoli, not forgetting to spoon over all the spicy, garlicky juices from the baking dish.

Pesto chicken & halloumi pasta

In just twenty minutes, and using only five ingredients, you'll get a tasty bowl of pasta that is bursting with pesto and halloumi flavours, sure to be a hit with everyone you cook it for. Halloumi is very popular and a lot of people go for lighter versions, which are fine to use here.

serves: **2**
prep time: **10 mins**
cook time: **10 mins**

200g pasta shapes (we used fusilli for the photo)
1 skinless chicken breast
150g cherry tomatoes, halved
225g halloumi cheese, the lighter type if you like, cut into 5mm slices
150g basil pesto

From the storecupboard
1 tablespoon olive oil
salt and black pepper

1. Cook the pasta in salted boiling water for 2 minutes less than the packet states. Drain, but reserve some of the cooking water.

2. Meanwhile, cut the chicken breast into bite-sized pieces and season with salt and pepper.

3. Heat the oil in a large frying pan over a medium-high heat. Cook the chicken until it's sealed, which means there are no visible pink bits. Add half the cherry tomatoes and cook for a couple more minutes, stirring occasionally.

4. Meanwhile, place another frying pan over a high heat, add the halloumi slices without any oil and cook until they are golden brown on each side. Once browned, remove from the pan and cover with foil to keep warm and soft.

5. Add a small ladle of pasta cooking water to the chicken and tomatoes, along with the drained pasta. Add the basil pesto and remaining cherry tomatoes and stir well. Ladle in a little more pasta water, if it needs loosening up. Taste and adjust the seasoning, remembering that the salty halloumi is still to be added, so you probably won't need any salt.

6. Dish up the pasta on to warmed plates and top with the seared halloumi to serve.

Teriyaki sirloin steak stir-fry

• • • • • • • • • • • • • • • •

Put the phone down, you don't need to call the takeaway tonight, because here's a recipe for a speedy and saucy teriyaki beef with the bare minimum of ingredients. Filled with tender sirloin steak and crisp veggies stirred through egg noodles, this really is lovely.

serves: **2**
prep time: **5 mins**
cook time: **10 mins**

300g sirloin steak
1 red pepper, sliced
80g mange tout, halved
   lengthways
80g spring onions, sliced
400g ready-cooked egg
   noodles
75ml teriyaki sauce (for
   homemade, see page 159)

From the storecupboard
1–2 tablespoons vegetable or
   sunflower oil
salt and black pepper

1. Season the steak with salt and pepper. Heat the oil in a wok or a large frying pan over a high heat. Sear the steak just until it's browned on both sides, then remove it from the pan and set aside.

2. Reduce the heat under the wok or pan to medium-high, then add the red pepper and mange tout. Stir-fry the vegetables for a couple of minutes until they start to soften.

3. Thinly slice the steak, then add it to the pan with most of the spring onions, the noodles, teriyaki sauce and a splash of water. Stir-fry for a few minutes to warm everything through.

4. Scatter with the remaining spring onions and serve.

Smoky bacon & Parmesan pasta

• • • • • • • • • • • • • • • • • • •

Pasta, bacon, cream, cheese: four of my favourite things all in one dish that's ready in less than twenty minutes. If you have a well-stocked fridge, you may well have all these ingredients to hand. (You can cut bacon rashers into chunks, if you don't have lardons.)

serves: **2**
prep time: **5 mins**
cook time: **15 mins**

200g spaghetti
150g smoked bacon lardons
  (or see recipe introduction)
½ onion, finely chopped
200ml double cream
40g finely grated Parmesan
  cheese
10g parsley leaves, chopped

From the storecupboard
salt and black pepper

1. Drop the pasta into salted boiling water and cook it for 2 minutes less than the packet states.

2. Meanwhile, in a large frying pan, fry the smoked bacon lardons over a medium-high heat until they start to turn crispy. Add the onion and cook it in the bacon fat for a couple more minutes.

3. Pour in a ladle of pasta cooking water, followed by the cream. Bring to the boil, then reduce the heat to a simmer. Add a pinch of black pepper and most of the Parmesan.

4. When the pasta is ready, use tongs to add it to the sauce. Stir it in briskly: this will knock some of the starch out of the pasta and thicken the sauce. If you need to loosen it up, add a bit of the pasta cooking water. Taste for seasoning and adjust it if needed.

5. Sprinkle in the parsley and stir it through, then serve, finishing with a grating of the remaining Parmesan over the top.

Chickpea & chorizo stew

. . . .

A hearty dish with spicy chorizo and basil pesto providing all the flavour. If you can, spend a bit more on some higher-quality chickpeas (those tend to be sold in jars), which will make all the difference in this recipe. You can switch the chickpeas for any other type of bean, too: cannellini or butter beans both work well.

serves: **4**
prep time: **5 mins**
cook time: **20 mins**

250g chorizo
1 onion, finely chopped
1 tablespoon tomato purée
2 × 400g cans of chopped
   tomatoes
2 × 400g cans of chickpeas,
   drained
80g basil pesto, plus more
   to serve

From the storecupboard
1 tablespoon olive oil
salt and black pepper

1. Slice the chorizo into 5mm chunks. Heat the oil in a pan over a medium-high heat and cook the chorizo for a few minutes until it starts to turn crispy.

2. Add the onion and cook for a few minutes until it softens. Add the tomato purée and continue to cook for a further minute.

3. Tip in the tomatoes and chickpeas, bring to the boil, then reduce the heat and simmer for 10 minutes.

4. Taste for seasoning, adjust that if necessary, then swirl through the pesto. Serve with more pesto on the side, with crusty bread or chunks of focaccia for dunking.

This chapter is packed with dishes that either conjure up a nostalgic feeling, or feel both cosy and hearty. They bring a sense of happiness, warmth, and – most of all – comfort! Often, comfort foods are slow-cooked dishes that take time to perfect, but in this chapter I've collected some of my favourites that come together quickly, without any fuss.

Quick
Comforts

Garlic butter chicken

• • • • • • • • • • • • • • • • • •

Garlic, butter and Parmesan are three of the most popular comforting ingredients – they will elevate any dish – and they are the main flavours in this indulgent, hug-in-a-bowl recipe. Serve it with any type of potatoes for extra comfort points – try my Crispy diced potatoes or Baby hasselbacks (see pages 14 and 13) – or with rice, and add salad or seasonal veggies.

serves: **2**
prep time: **5 mins**
cook time: **15 mins**

50g plain flour
1 teaspoon garlic granules
1 teaspoon salt
1 teaspoon black pepper
2 skinless chicken breasts
1–2 tablespoons vegetable or
   sunflower oil
1 onion, finely chopped
6 garlic cloves, finely chopped
200ml chicken stock
100g unsalted butter, chopped
30g finely grated Parmesan
   cheese
15g parsley leaves, chopped

1. Tip the flour into a bowl, add the garlic granules, salt and pepper and stir to coat.

2. Slice the chicken breasts in half lengthways to give 4 even-sized pieces. Coat the chicken in the seasoned flour.

3. Put the oil in a large frying pan over a medium-high heat. Cook the chicken for 3–4 minutes on each side until it's cooked through and golden all over. Remove from the pan, leaving the oil behind, and set aside.

4. Add the onion to the oil left in the pan and cook for a few minutes, until it starts to soften. Chuck in the garlic and cook for a further minute, before pouring in the stock.

5. Get the chicken back into the pan, reduce the heat to medium and bring to a simmer.

6. Add the butter, Parmesan and parsley and heat, stirring, until the butter and cheese have melted and the sauce has emulsified. (You may need to remove the chicken from the pan and beat or whisk the sauce to bring it together.) Taste for seasoning, adjusting it if needed, then serve.

Pictured with Crispy diced potatoes, see page 14.

Salmon, lemon & Parmesan orzo

• • • • • • • • • • • • • • • •

Tender fish cooked in creamy orzo with lemon and Parmesan: this is a really special dinner, yet it's fast to make and all cooked in one pan. Try it with dressed rocket, or garlic bread for even more comforting vibes.

serves: **4**
prep time: **10 mins**
cook time: **20 mins**

4 salmon fillets
1–2 tablespoons olive oil
20g unsalted butter
1 onion, finely chopped
4 garlic cloves, finely chopped
220g orzo
500ml vegetable stock
200g cherry tomatoes,
  quartered
80ml double cream
80g finely grated Parmesan
  cheese
finely grated zest and juice of
  1 lemon, plus lemon wedges
  (optional), to serve
leaves from a bunch of parsley,
  chopped
salt and black pepper

1. Season the salmon fillets with salt and pepper. Heat the oil and butter in a large frying pan.

2. Cook the fish skin side up over a medium heat for 3–4 minutes until the fillets are golden. Flip them over and fry skin side down for 1–2 minutes. Don't worry about the fish being fully cooked yet. Transfer to a plate and set aside, leaving the fat in the pan.

3. Using the same pan, cook the onion for a few minutes until it softens.

4. Add the garlic and cook for a further minute before tipping in the orzo. Give it a stir, now pour in the stock and pop the salmon fillets into the orzo with the cherry tomatoes.

5. Bring to the boil, then reduce the heat and simmer for 8–10 minutes, stirring occasionally, until the orzo is al dente and the fish is cooked. The heat should be gentle: you don't want to boil this.

6. Remove the fish while you pour in the cream, then add the Parmesan, lemon zest and juice. Stir well, then return the salmon.

7. Sprinkle over the chopped parsley, then season to taste. If it feels a little loose, leave it to stand for a minute or so, giving the orzo time to soak up the extra liquid, then serve with lemon wedges, if you like.

Potato, chicken & leek soup

Where curry meets the classic healing chicken soup: a proper warming bowlful that can be ready in thirty minutes. The chicken thighs pull apart beautifully to give the most delicious shredded meat. Serve this up with crusty bread, or Indian flatbreads, to soothe any seasonal sniffles.

serves: **4**
prep time: **5 mins**
cook time: **25 mins**

1 tablespoon vegetable or
  sunflower oil
1 onion, finely chopped
1 leek, sliced
4 garlic cloves, finely chopped
1 tablespoon curry powder
¼ teaspoon ground turmeric
600ml chicken stock
2 Maris Piper potatoes, peeled
  and chopped into 1cm cubes
400g skinless boneless
  chicken thighs
10g parsley leaves, finely chopped
1 lemon
salt and black pepper

1. Heat the oil in a heavy-based pan over a medium-high heat. Once the oil is hot, add the onion and leek and cook for about 5 minutes, or until they soften.

2. Add the garlic, curry powder and turmeric and cook for another minute until aromatic.

3. Pour in the chicken stock, then add the potatoes and chicken. Bring the soup to the boil, then reduce the heat to a simmer and cook until both the potatoes and chicken are cooked through and tender (this should not take more than 15–20 minutes).

4. Remove the chicken from the pan and set aside. Blend the soup until it's smooth, thick and creamy. (You may need to add more water, if you want to loosen the consistency.)

5. Use 2 forks to shred the chicken, then return it to the soup along with the parsley. Add the juice of half the lemon and taste for seasoning. As well as salt and pepper, you may want to add more lemon juice, to give the soup a little more acidity. Serve in warmed bowls.

Crispy Parmesan chicken

● ● ● ● ● ● ● ● ● ● ● ● ● ● ● ●

Italian-inspired comfort food at its best: crispy fried chicken topped with the familiar flavours of marinara sauce and mozzarella cheese. This recipe is my version of chicken parmigiana, a popular Italian dish. Serve with a lightly dressed rocket salad and garlic bread.

serves: **4**
prep time: **5 mins**
cook time: **25 mins**

For the marinara sauce
1 onion, finely chopped
1 tablespoon olive oil
4 garlic cloves, finely chopped
600ml tomato passata
2 teaspoons dried oregano

For the chicken
2 large skinless chicken breasts
50g plain flour
2 eggs, lightly beaten
60g breadcrumbs
120g finely grated Parmesan
  cheese
olive oil, to shallow-fry
80g grated mozzarella cheese
½ bunch of basil leaves, torn

1. To make the marinara sauce, fry the onion in a pan in the oil for a few minutes until it starts to soften. Add the garlic and cook for a further minute before pouring in the tomato passata and adding the oregano. Bring the sauce to a simmer and cook for 5 minutes over a medium heat.

2. Meanwhile, slice the chicken breasts in half lengthways.

3. Get together 3 bowls, the first with the flour, the second with the eggs and the last with the breadcrumbs. Add 80g of the the Parmesan to the breadcrumbs and mix it well. Coat the chicken in the flour, then in the eggs, then finally in the cheesy breadcrumbs.

4. Heat up a good amount of oil in a frying pan over a medium-high heat; you need enough oil to come halfway up the sides of the coated chicken pieces. Shallow-fry the chicken until it's crispy and golden on both sides and cooked all the way through. Pop it on to a plate lined with kitchen paper to blot off the excess oil.

5. Preheat the grill to high.

6. Pour two-thirds of the marinara sauce into a large roasting dish that you can put under the grill, then place the chicken on top. Spoon over the remaining sauce. Sprinkle the grated mozzarella on top of the chicken, followed by a scattering of torn basil leaves and the remaining grated Parmesan.

7. Pop it under the hot grill until the cheese melts, then serve.

Creamy chorizo gnocchi

• • • • • • • • • • • • • • • •

Worthy of a place in your midweek repertoire, this is the ultimate one-pot meal after a busy day and it's ready in less than twenty minutes. Chorizo is a near-universally popular Spanish sausage with lots of garlic and paprika inside it, which helps both elevate the flavour and enrich this recipe.

serves: **2**
prep time: **10 mins**
cook time: **10 mins**

1 tablespoon olive oil
150g chorizo, chopped
1 small red onion, finely chopped
1 small red pepper, chopped
4 garlic cloves, finely chopped
150ml chicken stock
1 tablespoon tomato purée
100g cream cheese
400g gnocchi
40g finely grated Parmesan
  cheese, plus more to serve
25g basil leaves, torn
salt and black pepper

1. Heat the oil in a large frying pan, then cook the chorizo over a medium-high heat for a few minutes until it starts to turn crispy.

2. Add the red onion and red pepper and cook until they soften, about 4 minutes.

3. Chuck in the garlic and cook for a minute before pouring in the chicken stock, then add the tomato purée, cream cheese and gnocchi. Stir well, then reduce the heat to medium. Cover with a lid or a sheet of foil and simmer for 4–5 minutes until the gnocchi is tender and the sauce has thickened.

4. Add the Parmesan and basil leaves and stir well. Taste for seasoning, adjusting it if necessary, then serve the gnocchi with more grated Parmesan.

Smoky chipotle chicken

• • • • • • • • • • • • • • • • • • •

Chicken in a warm, smoky tomato sauce, great with rice or crispy potatoes and tortilla chips. Chipotles are common in Mexican cooking; use them whenever you want to add a real smoky heat to food. This is bound to be a smash hit recipe, especially on those nights when everyone needs a lift.

serves: **4**
prep time: **5 mins**
cook time: **25 mins**

80g plain flour
2 teaspoons salt
2 teaspoons black pepper
4 skinless chicken breasts
2 tablespoons vegetable or
  sunflower oil
25g unsalted butter
1 onion, finely chopped
1 green pepper, finely chopped
6 garlic cloves, finely chopped
1 tablespoon ground cumin
2 tablespoons smoked paprika
  (not hot smoked)
1 tablespoon tomato purée
2 tablespoons chipotle paste
400g can of chopped
  tomatoes
400g can of black beans,
  drained
20g coriander, chopped

To serve (optional)
soured cream
lime wedges

1. Put the flour, salt and pepper in a bowl and mix it well. Coat the chicken breasts in the seasoned flour.

2. Heat the oil in a large frying pan over a medium-high heat. Add the butter and, when it melts, cook the chicken until it's golden brown on both sides.

3. Remove the chicken from the pan, leaving the buttery oil behind, and set aside. Add the onion and green pepper to the pan and cook for about 5 minutes or until the vegetables soften.

4. Chuck in the garlic, cumin, smoked paprika, tomato purée and chipotle paste and cook for a couple of minutes to release the flavours and aromas.

5. Pour in the can of tomatoes, then fill the can half-full with water and add that, too, along with the black beans. Get the chicken back into the pan and coat it in the sauce. Bring it to the boil, then reduce the heat and simmer for 8–10 minutes.

6. Stir through the chopped coriander and taste for seasoning, adjusting that if necessary. Serve the chicken with a bowl of soured cream and lime wedges, if you like.

Watt's the Story?

All chipotle chillies start as jalapeños, which are left on the plant to ripen until semi-sweet and ruby-red. Once they reach that point, they are dried and lightly smoked, to give deliciously smoky chipotles.

Honey-mustard sausages & mash

The undisputed king of British comfort foods, especially when paired with a delicious and creamy honey-mustard sauce. Dish it up with mash (of course) and seasonal veg (we used steamed spring greens for the photo).

serves: **2**
prep time: **10 mins**
cook time: **20 mins**

1–2 tablespoons vegetable or sunflower oil
6 good-quality sausages, ideally higher-welfare
1 onion, finely chopped
2 garlic cloves, finely chopped
100ml chicken stock
2 tablespoons honey
2 tablespoons wholegrain mustard
150ml double cream
leaves from a small bunch of parsley, chopped
salt and black pepper

1. Heat the oil in a large frying pan over a medium-high heat. Fry the sausages until they are browned all over.

2. Remove the sausages from the pan, leaving the oil behind, and set aside. Reduce the heat under the pan to medium, put the onion in and cook for about 5 minutes until it starts to soften.

3. Add the garlic and cook for a further minute.

4. Pour in the stock, then add the honey and mustard and bring the pan to the boil. Pour in the cream and get the sausages back in there. Give it a stir and cook it for a few minutes, stirring occasionally, until the sauce thickens.

5. Add the parsley, then taste for seasoning, adjusting if necessary, and serve with mash.

Pictured with Simple mashed potato, see page 15.

Hunter's chicken

•••••••••••••••••••••

A British pub classic: chicken breast wrapped in bacon, smothered with barbecue sauce and topped with melted cheese. Dish it up with potatoes; traditionally it would come with chunky chips. It's one of those recipes that everyone knows and loves: a good midweek friend.

serves: **2**
prep time: **5 mins**
cook time: **25 mins**

2 skinless chicken breasts
½ teaspoon salt
½ teaspoon black pepper
1 teaspoon paprika (not hot)
1 teaspoon garlic granules
1 tablespoon olive oil
6 streaky bacon rashers
4 tablespoons barbecue sauce
80g grated Cheddar cheese

1. Preheat the oven to 200°C fan.

2. Place the chicken in a mixing bowl, then add the salt, pepper, paprika, garlic granules and olive oil. Mix well to coat the chicken.

3. Wrap each chicken breast in 3 rashers of streaky bacon, then place in a baking dish. Bake for 20 minutes, or until golden and cooked through. (If you want to check, slice into the thickest part of the chicken: you should see no trace of pink. If you do, cook for a few minutes more, then test again.)

4. Spoon over the barbecue sauce evenly, spreading it liberally over the chicken. Sprinkle over the Cheddar, then pop the baking dish back into the oven for 5 minutes, until the cheese is nicely melted. Serve it straight away, while it's bubbling-hot.

Meatball stroganoff

• • • • • • • • • • • • • • • • • •

This rich and flavourful recipe is the perfect weeknight dinner when you need a little treat: mushrooms and meatballs swimming in an indulgently creamy sauce. Cooking stroganoff with meatballs rather than steak makes it more fun and a little bit more child-friendly too, if you have young kids to feed. This works brilliantly with either rice or mashed potato.

serves: **4**
prep time: **10 mins**
cook time: **20 mins**

For the meatballs
500g minced beef
60g breadcrumbs
1 egg, lightly beaten
1 tablespoon paprika (not hot)
1 teaspoon salt
1 teaspoon black pepper
1–2 tablespoons vegetable or
  sunflower oil

For the sauce
1 onion, finely chopped
250g chestnut mushrooms,
  quartered
4 garlic cloves, finely chopped
200ml beef stock
180g half-fat crème fraîche
1 tablespoon Dijon mustard
15g parsley leaves, chopped

1. Put the minced beef in a large mixing bowl with the breadcrumbs, egg, paprika, salt and pepper. Get stuck in and mix it until it's well combined. Roll the mixture into 16 equal-sized meatballs.

2. Heat the oil in a large frying pan over a medium-high heat. Fry the meatballs until they are golden brown all over, then remove from the pan, leaving the oil behind, and set aside.

3. Using the same pan, cook the onion for 4–5 minutes until it starts to soften. Add the mushrooms and cook for a couple of minutes, then add the garlic and cook for a further minute.

4. Pour in the stock, then add the crème fraîche and Dijon mustard. Stir well, then get the meatballs back in the pan.

5. Bring to the boil and cook until the sauce thickens and the meatballs are cooked through. (If you cut into a meatball, there should be no trace of pink. If there is, continue to cook for another couple of minutes, then test again.)

6. Season to taste, then stir through the parsley and serve.

Chicken & chorizo risotto

• • • • • • • • • • • • • • • • •

Both Spain and Italy would probably be angry with me for this recipe, but it's too good not to share! It's already been a hit online: the tender chicken, spicy chorizo and creamy, cheesy risotto rice are a match made in heaven. Thank me later.

serves: **2**
prep time: **5 mins**
cook time: **25 mins**

1 tablespoon olive oil
120g chorizo, finely chopped,
   plus chorizo slices (optional)
   to serve
2 skinless boneless chicken
   thighs, cut into chunks
1 onion, finely chopped
150g risotto rice
500ml chicken stock
30g unsalted butter, chopped
30g finely grated Parmesan
   cheese, plus more to serve
10g parsley leaves, chopped
salt and black pepper

1. Heat the oil in a large frying pan and cook the chopped chorizo and chicken over a high heat for about 5 minutes, until the chicken is sealed all over (with no visible bits of pink) and the chorizo starts to turn crispy.

2. Use a slotted spoon to remove the chicken and chorizo from the pan and set aside. If you want to serve this with crispy chorizo slices, now's the time to crisp them up in the pan, again using a slotted spoon to remove them once they're done. Keep the oil in the pan.

3. Chuck the onion into the red chorizo oil and cook until it softens, then add the rice and cook for a further few minutes, stirring continuously.

4. Pour in the stock, then get the chicken and chopped chorizo back in the pan (not the slices, reserve those, if you used them). Simmer for 15 minutes, stirring occasionally, until the stock has been absorbed.

5. Add the butter and Parmesan and stir well. Once the butter melts, stir through the parsley, then taste for seasoning.

6. Dish it up in warmed bowls, then finish with more grated Parmesan and the crispy chorizo slices, if you like.

Hawaiian pork chops

This sweet-and-sour sauce is exactly the same as the type you can buy in tubs and pouches, but made at home. You'll be surprised at how easy it is and you might find you won't need to buy it ready-made again. Add some rice and seasonal veggies on the side, if you like.

serves: **4**
prep time: **5 mins**
cook time: **20 mins**

4 boneless pork chops
1–2 tablespoons vegetable or sunflower oil
1 red onion, sliced
1 red pepper, sliced
80ml soy sauce
3 tablespoons tomato ketchup
50g soft brown sugar
435g can of pineapple slices in juice
4 garlic cloves, finely chopped
15g root ginger, finely grated
1 tablespoon cornflour
2 tablespoons water
coriander leaves, to serve (optional)
salt and black pepper

1. Season the chops with salt and pepper. Heat the oil in a frying pan over a medium-high heat and cook the pork for 2–3 minutes on each side until browned.

2. Remove the chops from the pan, leaving the oil behind, and set aside. Add the sliced onion and red pepper to the same pan and cook for a couple of minutes until they start to soften.

3. Meanwhile, in a bowl or a jug, mix the soy sauce, ketchup, sugar, pineapple juice (reserve the slices), garlic and ginger. Pour this sauce into the pan, then get the pork chops back in there. Flip the chops over a few times to coat them in the sauce.

4. Add 4 slices of pineapple to the pan, then bring it to a simmer and cook for 4–5 minutes, turning the chops over halfway through.

5. Mix the cornflour in a cup or small bowl with the measured water, then stir this into the sauce bit by bit, stirring constantly, until it thickens to the consistency you'd like. (It might help to remove the pineapple and pork from the pan while you do this.)

6. Serve the chops with the sauce, topping each with a pineapple slice and a few coriander leaves, if you like.

Crispy chilli chicken

● ● ● ● ● ● ● ● ● ● ● ● ● ● ● ● ●

This sweet and spicy stir-fry went viral for me on social media a little while back. It is a version of the famous Chinese crispy chilli beef dish, but made with chicken, which is so hugely popular. (One of the questions I am always asked, when I publish a pork or beef recipe, is whether it can be made with chicken!) Though it may look exotic, the recipe uses ingredients that you may well already have in the cupboard. Lovely over fluffy jasmine rice.

serves: **2**
prep time: **10 mins**
cook time: **15 mins**

1 head of broccoli
2 skinless chicken breasts
3 tablespoons cornflour
1 tablespoon vegetable or
  sunflower oil
1 red chilli, sliced
2 teaspoons garlic paste
2 teaspoons ginger paste
4 tablespoons soy sauce
2 tablespoons honey
juice of 1 lime
2 tablespoons sweet chilli
  sauce

To serve (optional)
2 spring onions, shredded
1 red chilli, sliced

1. Cut the broccoli into florets, then drop them into boiling water for a couple of minutes until tender. Drain and set aside.

2. Cut the chicken breasts into strips, then pop into a bowl and toss in the cornflour until completely coated.

3. Put the oil into a large frying pan over a medium-high heat and fry the chicken for 5–6 minutes until golden and crispy all over.

4. Add the chilli and the garlic and ginger pastes and stir-fry for a minute before adding the broccoli. Stir-fry for another minute.

5. Now add the soy sauce, honey, lime juice and sweet chilli sauce. Cook until the sauce starts to thicken.

6. Serve scattered with shredded spring onions and chilli, if you like.

Spanish-style chicken stew

● ● ● ● ● ● ● ● ● ● ● ● ● ● ● ● ● ● ●

A quick, satisfying dish that combines the smoky Spanish flavours of paprika and chorizo and is good with rice, potato wedges or even just a chunk of crusty bread.

serves: **2**
prep time: **5 mins**
cook time: **20 mins**

1 tablespoon olive oil
150g chorizo, chopped
1 onion, finely chopped
2 garlic cloves, finely chopped
1½ tablespoons smoked
   paprika (not hot smoked)
400g can of chopped
   tomatoes
1 tablespoon tomato purée
400g skinless boneless chicken
   thighs, chopped into bite-
   sized pieces
10g parsley leaves, chopped
salt and black pepper

1. Heat the oil in a large frying pan over a medium-high heat. Add the chorizo and cook for a few minutes until it starts to turn crispy. Now add the onion and cook for a few more minutes until it softens. Chuck in the garlic and paprika and cook for a further minute.

2. Pour in the can of chopped tomatoes and the tomato purée. Get the chicken straight into the pan and stir well.

3. Bring to the boil, then cover with a lid or a sheet of foil and simmer for 10–12 minutes, or until the chicken is cooked through. (If you cut into a larger piece of chicken, the juices should run clear. If not, continue to cook for another couple of minutes, then test again.)

4. Stir through the parsley, then taste for seasoning, adjusting that as needed, and serve.

Pictured with Cajun-spiced potato wedges, see page 13.

Watt's the Story?

Watch out for tomatoes that have been canned in an over-acidic juice, as they can let down recipes. If your tomatoes are a bit acidic, you can add a teaspoon of sugar to balance it out. Good-quality tomatoes – I like the Mutti brand – won't have this souring effect and contain more vitamin C than you imagine, too.

Chilli con carne

You'd be forgiven for assuming this classic recipe is a Mexican dish. There is certainly a Mexican influence, but it actually comes from Texas in the southern United States. It's the perfect warming meal, especially in the colder months. This recipe contains chocolate; I know that sounds weird, but trust me, it adds the perfect amount of sweet richness (and even more comfort). Dish this up with rice, or sweet potato wedges.

serves: **4**
prep time: **5 mins**
cook time: **25 mins**

1–2 tablespoons vegetable or
   sunflower oil
1 onion, finely chopped
1 red pepper, finely chopped
500g minced beef
4 garlic cloves, finely chopped
1 teaspoon paprika (not hot)
1 teaspoon ground cumin
2 teaspoons dried oregano
1 teaspoon chilli powder
1 tablespoon chipotle paste
1 tablespoon tomato purée
400g can of chopped
   tomatoes
200ml beef stock
400g can of butter beans,
   drained
20g dark chocolate, 70% cocoa
   solids, broken up
salt and black pepper

To serve (optional)
soured cream
coriander leaves

1. Heat the oil in a large frying pan. Fry the onion and red pepper over a medium-high heat until they soften.

2. Add the minced beef and use a wooden spoon or spatula to break it up as much as you can. Cook, stirring and breaking it up again, until it's browned all over.

3. Chuck in the garlic, paprika, cumin, oregano, chilli powder, chipotle paste and tomato purée and cook for 2 more minutes. Pour in the can of tomatoes and the stock, bring to the boil, then reduce the heat and simmer for about 10 minutes.

4. Add the drained butter beans, stir well, then add the chocolate. Stir it through, then simmer for a further 10 minutes.

5. Taste for seasoning, adjust as needed, then serve with your choice of sides, a dollop of soured cream and a scattering of coriander, if you like.

Step into a world where indulgence meets balance, with a whole chapter dedicated to speedy low-calorie, delicious midweek meals. I've tried to major on those flavours you might be craving when you cut back, to help you keep your resolutions. Whether you're looking to maintain a healthy lifestyle, lose weight, or simply enjoy food that is light on calories but heavy on taste, these are for you.

Low
Calorie

Egg-fried rice

• • • • • • • • • • • • • • • • • •

A simple, healthy way to enjoy a quick meal that can too often be filled with oil. You can use 190g leftover cold rice, or rice from a shop-bought pouch, or leave freshly cooked rice to dry out before using, to stop it sticking to the wok. And don't worry about the safety of pre-cooked rice; at home, if you cool, cover and chill rice promptly, it will be good to eat for a couple of days.

serves: **2**
prep time: **10 mins**
cook time: **10 mins**

80g basmati rice
1 tablespoon vegetable or
   sunflower oil
½ red pepper, sliced
60g spring onions, sliced
120g raw shelled king prawns,
   halved lengthways
80g sliced ham, cut into chunks
50g frozen peas
1 tablespoon soy sauce
2 large eggs, lightly beaten
10g coriander, chopped
   (optional)
salt and black pepper

405 calories per portion

1. Cook the rice according to the packet instructions, then drain. Leave to get cold (ideally), or at least to dry out, before using.

2. Heat the oil in a wok or a large frying pan over a high heat. Add the red pepper and most of the spring onions and cook for a minute.

3. Add the cooked rice, prawns, ham, peas and soy sauce and stir-fry for a few minutes, until the prawns are pink.

4. Stir in the beaten eggs and cook for another minute, stirring all the time, until they scramble.

5. Sprinkle in most of the coriander, if using, stir it through and taste for seasoning, adjusting that if needed.

6. Serve sprinkled with the remaining spring onions and the rest of the coriander, if you want.

Pasta alla puttanesca

• • • • • • • • • • • • • • • • •

A pasta dish from Naples, which is both healthy and utterly satisfying, due to its big, mouth-filling flavours. You can leave out the anchovies if you want, but trust me when I say they add so much flavour: they melt into the sauce too, so you won't notice them.

serves: **4**
prep time: **5 mins**
cook time: **15 mins**

1 teaspoon olive oil
1 onion, finely chopped
2 garlic cloves, sliced
1 red chilli, sliced
4 anchovy fillets, chopped
400g can of chopped
  tomatoes
120g pitted Kalamata olives
  (drained weight)
20g capers (drained weight),
  rinsed if needed
320g pasta shapes (we used
  conchiglie for the photo)
100g cherry tomatoes, halved
10g parsley leaves, chopped
40g rocket
salt

429 calories per portion

1. Heat the oil in a large frying pan over a medium-high heat. Add the onion and cook until it softens.

2. Chuck in the garlic, chilli and anchovy fillets and cook for a further minute until aromatic.

3. Add the canned tomatoes, olives and capers and bring to the boil. Simmer for 10 minutes.

4. Meanwhile, cook the pasta in salted boiling water for 2 minutes less than the packet states. Once cooked, drain it, but reserve some of the pasta water.

5. Add the drained pasta to the sauce and use some of its cooking water to loosen it up, if needed.

6. Stir through the cherry tomatoes and parsley, then serve with the rocket leaves on the side, or stirred through to wilt.

Chinese chicken curry

• • • • • • • • • • • • • • • • • •

A British takeaway classic, you can cook this streamlined curry in only fifteen minutes, making it much quicker than the average delivery service! There's no cream here, as the sauce is stock-based, and it's also filled with vegetables, so it's not your typical rich, calorific, heavy curry.

serves: **2**
prep time: **5 mins**
cook time: **15 mins**

2 skinless chicken breasts, cut into bite-sized pieces
2 tablespoons soy sauce
1 tablespoon cornflour
1 teaspoon Chinese five spice
1 teaspoon vegetable or sunflower oil
1 onion, sliced
2 garlic cloves, finely chopped
10g root ginger, very finely chopped or finely grated
2 tablespoons curry powder
300ml chicken stock
1 red pepper, sliced
80g mange tout
120g cooked white rice, to serve

519 calories per portion, including 60g cooked white rice per portion (see below)

1. Put the chicken in a mixing bowl, then add the soy sauce, cornflour and Chinese five spice. Stir to coat.

2. Heat the oil in a wok or a large frying pan over a medium-high heat. Stir-fry the onion for a few minutes until it softens.

3. Add the garlic, ginger and curry powder and cook for a further minute, until aromatic.

4. Now tip in the coated chicken, pour in the stock, stir well and simmer for 10 minutes, stirring occasionally.

5. Add the sliced pepper and mange tout, then cook for a few more minutes, until the vegetables soften.

6. Dish the curry up in warmed bowls with the rice.

Watt's the Story?

It's useful to know that the weight of white rice will slightly more than double once it's cooked. So the 120g total of cooked white rice served here, between two people, would need you to cook 50g raw white rice, according to the packet instructions.

Lighter beef stroganoff

• • • • • • • • • • • • • • • •

A way to carry on enjoying steak within a healthy regime. Stroganoff is arguably one of the most popular comfort foods and my lighter version doesn't scrimp on flavour, despite getting rid of the traditional cream, as the yogurt in the sauce makes it creamy. You can serve this with mashed potatoes or pasta instead of rice, but those will both increase the calories.

serves: **2**
prep time: **10 mins**
cook time: **15 mins**

300g sirloin steak
1 teaspoon vegetable or
    sunflower oil
1 onion, sliced
150g chestnut mushrooms,
    sliced
10g unsalted butter
1 tablespoon plain flour
1 tablespoon paprika (not hot)
240ml beef stock
1 tablespoon Worcestershire
    sauce
1 teaspoon Dijon mustard
2 tablespoons Greek-style
    yogurt, or natural yogurt
10g parsley leaves, chopped
120g cooked white rice, to serve
salt and black pepper

586 calories per portion, including 60g cooked white rice per portion (see page 115)

1. Trim the fat off the steak, then cut the meat into thin slices.

2. Heat the oil in a large frying pan over a high heat. Season the beef with salt and pepper, then cook just until it's browned all over, but don't cook it any further as you want it to stay juicy. Remove the beef from the pan with a slotted spoon, leaving the oil behind, and set aside.

3. Reduce the heat under the pan to medium-high. Cook the onion and mushrooms for about 5 minutes, until they start to soften.

4. Once soft, add the butter, then, when it melts, add the flour and paprika, stir well and cook for 1 more minute.

5. Pour in the stock and stir well. Add the Worcestershire sauce and Dijon mustard and cook until the sauce has thickened slightly.

6. Get the beef back into the pan along with any of its juices, then stir through the yogurt and parsley, leaving it marbled through if you like. Taste for seasoning, adjust if needed, then serve with the rice.

Coconut lime chicken

• • • • • • • • • • • • • • • • • •

A Thai-style chicken that is low-calorie by accident, this is delicious, super-quick and easy, so it's sure to become a regular on your dinner table. Tasty, but with only a handful of ingredients, the lime and fish sauce add really mouth-filling, powerful flavours, so you won't feel you're missing out.

serves: **2**
prep time: **10 mins**
cook time: **15 mins**

2 skinless chicken breasts
1½ teaspoons vegetable or
   sunflower oil
1 onion, finely chopped
4 garlic cloves, finely chopped
15g root ginger, very finely
   chopped or finely grated
1 red chilli, sliced
finely grated zest and juice of
   2 limes, plus more lime zest
   and lime wedges (optional)
   to serve
200ml light coconut milk
2 teaspoons fish sauce
25g Thai basil leaves, chopped
120g cooked white rice, to serve

548 calories per portion, including
60g cooked white rice per portion
(see page 115)

1. Slice the chicken breasts in half lengthways to give 4 thinner pieces.

2. Heat the oil in a large frying pan over a medium-high heat. Cook the chicken until it's browned on both sides, then remove it from the pan with a slotted spoon, leaving the oil behind, and set aside.

3. Cook the chopped onion in the same pan for a few minutes until it has softened.

4. Once soft, chuck in the garlic, ginger, chilli and lime zest and cook for a further minute. Pour in the coconut milk, bring to the boil, then reduce the heat and simmer for a couple of minutes.

5. Get the chicken back into the pan along with any juices and cook for a couple more minutes.

6. Stir through the fish sauce and Thai basil, then taste for seasoning. Add as much lime juice as you think tastes good. Dish it up with the rice and add lime wedges and a scattering of lime zest, if you like.

Beef ramen

• • • • • • • • • • • • • • • • • •

This recipe uses minced beef, making it easier and more budget-friendly than the traditional sliced meat. Cooked in a sweet and savoury sauce with a tangle of noodles, it is both healthy and totally slurp-worthy.

serves: **2**
prep time: **5 mins**
cook time: **15 mins**

1 teaspoon vegetable or
  sunflower oil
250g extra-lean minced beef
½ onion, sliced
2 garlic cloves, finely chopped
15g root ginger, very finely
  chopped or finely grated
750ml beef stock
2 tablespoons soy sauce
1 tablespoon honey
150g sugar snap peas
140g dried fine egg noodles
50g spring onions, sliced
1 red chilli, sliced (optional)

540 calories per portion

1. Heat the oil in a large saucepan over a medium-high heat. Add the minced beef and cook until it's browned all over, stirring and breaking it up with a spoon. Remove the minced beef from the pan with a slotted spoon, leaving the fat in the pan, and set aside.

2. Add the onion to the same pan with the garlic and ginger and cook for 2 minutes.

3. Get the minced beef back into the pan, then pour in the stock. Bring to the boil, then reduce the heat and simmer for 5 minutes.

4. Add the soy sauce, honey, sugar snap peas and noodles. Cook for 3–4 minutes, or until the noodles are tender, trying to keep the noodles and sugar snaps under the surface of the liquid.

5. Divide between 2 warmed bowls, sprinkle with spring onions and serve. If you enjoy a bit of heat, then scatter over the sliced chilli too.

Chicken balti

• • • • • • • • • • • • • • • • • •

Here's how to make a lighter version of the Indian classic. Choose your curry powder depending on either what you have in the cupboard, or the heat you want, opting for mild for younger children or hot for chilli heads. It can be quite illuminating to read the ingredients on a tub of curry powder, because there's a lot more in there than you might think...

serves: **2**
prep time: **5 mins**
cook time: **25 mins**

1 teaspoon vegetable or
   sunflower oil
1 onion, sliced
300g skinless boneless chicken
   thighs, chopped into bite-
   sized pieces
2 mixed peppers, cut into
   chunks
1 tablespoon curry powder
   (see recipe introduction)
1 garlic clove, sliced
1 tablespoon tomato purée
small (227g) can of tomatoes
140g low-fat Greek yogurt
10g coriander, chopped
120g cooked white rice, to serve
salt and black pepper

608 calories per portion, including 60g cooked white rice per portion (see page 115)

1. Heat the oil in a large frying pan over a medium-high heat. Add the onion and cook until it softens and starts to brown.

2. Tip in the chicken and cook until it is sealed (there are no more visible pink bits).

3. Now add the peppers and cook for 2 more minutes.

4. Sprinkle in the curry powder, add the garlic and tomato purée and cook for a further minute.

5. Add the canned tomatoes and yogurt and simmer for 15 minutes, stirring occasionally, until the chicken is tender and the sauce is thick.

6. Stir through the coriander and taste for seasoning, then dish it up with the rice.

We all want to make the most of our evenings, particularly during the busy working week, so fuss-free dinners are a real game-changer. To me, that means it's essential to minimise time spent washing up after cooking, too. So here's a chapter of speedy recipes all made using a single pot, pan or roasting tray.

Speedy
One-Pot

One-pan penne n cheese

• • • • • • • • • • • • • • • • •

You won't believe how easy this speedy version of mac n cheese is until you've made it; I love it and I know you will too. The recipe revolutionises the regular mac n cheese technique, cutting a lot of the usual corners: just throw everything in one pan for an end-product dinner of creamy cheesy pasta goodness! It's good for kids, as the broccoli breaks up so there aren't any big chunks of green to put them off. Serve it with garlic bread on the side, of course.

serves: **2**
prep time: **5 mins**
cook time: **15 mins**

250g penne, or other
  pasta shapes
500ml water
200ml whole milk
1 head of broccoli, cut into florets
150g grated Cheddar cheese
80g finely grated Parmesan
  cheese
80g mascarpone, or cream
  cheese
½ teaspoon ground nutmeg

To serve (optional)
pancetta slices
chopped chives

1. Put the pasta, measured water, milk and broccoli into a pot and cover with a lid. Cook over a medium heat for 10–12 minutes, stirring occasionally, until the pasta is ready.

2. Meanwhile, if you want to serve this with pancetta, cook the slices in a dry frying pan until crispy, then set aside.

3. Once the pasta is cooked, stir in the Cheddar, Parmesan, mascarpone or cream cheese and nutmeg until all the cheeses have melted and the sauce is smooth.

4. Serve straight away, with the crispy pancetta and chopped chives scattered on top, if you like.

Spring salmon & greens traybake

I often play football on a Monday night and this is one of my favourite meals to make when I get home. I bang it all into a roasting tray, then jump in the shower while it's cooking. If you want to add carbs for the hungrier souls, sticky rice would work well, or just serve with crusty bread.

serves: **4**
prep time: **5 mins**
cook time: **20 mins**

200g Tenderstem broccoli
150g asparagus spears
200g sugar snap peas
150g frozen peas
2 tablespoons toasted sesame oil
4 salmon fillets, ideally skinless
2 tablespoons soy sauce
2 tablespoons honey
salt

For the dressing
15g root ginger, finely grated
2 spring onions, sliced
1 tablespoon toasted
  sesame oil
finely grated zest and juice
  of 1 lime
1 red chilli, finely sliced
  (optional)

1. Preheat the oven to 180°C fan.

2. Put the broccoli in a large roasting tray with the asparagus, sugar snaps and peas. Drizzle over the sesame oil and sprinkle over some salt. Toss to coat.

3. Nestle the salmon fillets on top of the vegetables.

4. In a small bowl, mix the soy sauce with the honey, then spoon it over each salmon fillet.

5. Bake for 20 minutes.

6. Meanwhile, make the dressing by mixing all the ingredients.

7. Once the salmon is cooked, spoon over the dressing and serve straight away.

Smoky spiced chicken & rice

· · · · · · · · · · · · · · · · · · ·

Chicken, spices, rice and vegetables all cooked in one pot, like a celebration of all the most delicious ingredients. This recipe is great even if you're only serving a couple of you, as you can stick the leftovers in a box in the fridge and eat it for your lunch the next day.

serves: **4**
prep time: **5 mins**
cook time: **25 mins**

500g skinless boneless
  chicken thighs
3 tablespoons olive oil
240g basmati rice
500ml chicken stock
1 carrot, finely chopped
100g frozen peas
1 lemon, plus lemon slices
  (optional) to serve
25g parsley leaves, chopped

For the spice mix
1 tablespoon smoked paprika
  (not hot smoked)
1 teaspoon garlic granules
1 teaspoon ground cumin
1 teaspoon cayenne pepper
1 teaspoon dried oregano, or
  mixed herbs
½ teaspoon ground turmeric
  (this is just for colour)
1 teaspoon salt

1. Put all the spice mix ingredients into a bowl and – well – mix!

2. Cut the chicken into bite-sized pieces and pop it into a bowl. Add half the spice mix with 2 tablespoons of the oil and stir to coat.

3. Heat the remaining 1 tablespoon of oil in a heavy-based pan over a medium-high heat. Cook the chicken for a few minutes until it's browned all over.

4. Add the rice, stock, carrot and the remaining spice mix and stir well. Cover and cook for 20 minutes or until the liquid is absorbed and the rice is tender.

5. Add the peas, the juice of half the lemon and the parsley and stir it through. Taste and add more lemon juice, if you want. Decorate with lemon slices if you like, then eat up.

Chicken & pancetta gnocchi

• • • • • • • • • • • • • •

Until I started cooking for a living, I hadn't heard of gnocchi. These Italian potato dumplings, sold in the chiller cabinet alongside the fresh pasta, are certainly becoming more popular at home. That's great news for our midweek dinners as – just like pasta – gnocchi can be served with an endless variety of sauces. And, of course, this is all cooked in a single pan.

serves: **4**
prep time: **5 mins**
cook time: **15 mins**

250g pancetta lardons
2 skinless chicken breasts,
  finely sliced
5 garlic cloves, finely chopped
300ml chicken stock
200ml double cream
2 teaspoons paprika (not hot)
800g gnocchi
60g finely grated Parmesan
  cheese, plus more to serve
125g parsley leaves, chopped
salt and black pepper

1. Put the pancetta into a large frying pan without any oil (it will release its own fat). Cook over a medium-high heat until it is starting to turn crispy. Add the chicken and cook until it's sealed, which means no more pink bits on the outside. Chuck in the garlic and cook for a further minute, then pour in the stock and cream and add the paprika. Stir well.

2. Add the gnocchi to the chicken and sauce and mix gently but well, then cover the pan with a lid or a sheet of foil. Simmer everything for 3–4 minutes, or until the sauce is creamy and coats the gnocchi.

3. Remove the lid, then sprinkle in the Parmesan and parsley. Mix well, then taste for seasoning and adjust if necessary. Take it to the table in warmed bowls, with more grated Parmesan.

Harissa chicken & Med veg bake

• • • • • • • • • • • • • • •

Loaded with roasted veggies and chicken, for big flavours with minimal effort. Rose harissa is the star of the show here; regular harissa will work too, but the rose variety takes this recipe to the next level. Traybakes are perfect for midweek meals, as you can get on with life as they tick away on their own in the oven.

serves: **4**
prep time: **5 mins**
cook time: **25 mins**

1 red pepper
1 red onion
1 courgette
1 aubergine
400g can of chickpeas, drained
3 tablespoons rose harissa
finely grated zest and juice of
  1 lemon
500g skinless boneless
  chicken thighs
100g Greek yogurt
salt and black pepper
mint leaves, to serve (optional)

1. Preheat the oven to 200°C fan.

2. Cut the pepper, onion, courgette and aubergine into chunks. Pop them into a bowl, then add the chickpeas, 2 tablespoons of the harissa and the lemon juice. (Reserve the lemon zest for now.)

3. Give it a good stir to coat, then tip it all into a large baking dish. Cook for 5 minutes.

4. Meanwhile, put the chicken into the empty bowl and add the remaining 1 tablespoon of harissa along with the Greek yogurt and some salt and pepper. Stir until coated.

5. Nestle the chicken on top and among the vegetables and bake for a further 20 minutes. To check it is cooked, slice into the thickest part of the chicken: you should see no trace of pink. If you do, cook for a few minutes more, then test again

6. Season to taste, then scatter over the lemon zest and sprinkle with mint leaves, if you like. Take the dish to the table and serve.

Lemony chicken orzo

A classic combination of flavours, with lemon zest and juice balancing the cream, and spinach providing the vitamins. You can substitute the spinach for shredded spring greens, if that's what you've got in the fridge.

serves: **4**
prep time: **5 mins**
cook time: **20 mins**

500g skinless boneless
   chicken thighs
25g unsalted butter
1 tablespoon olive oil
1 onion, finely chopped
4 garlic cloves, finely chopped
500ml chicken stock
250ml double cream
250g orzo
100g baby spinach
60g finely grated Parmesan
   cheese
finely grated zest and juice of
   1 lemon
salt and black pepper

1. Cut the chicken into small bite-sized pieces.

2. Heat the butter and oil in a large frying pan over a medium-high heat. Add the chicken and cook, stirring, until there are no more visible pink bits.

3. Add the onion and continue to cook for a few more minutes until it starts to soften.

4. Chuck in the garlic and cook for a further minute before pouring in the stock and cream.

5. Stir in the orzo, bring to the boil, then reduce the heat to a simmer; don't rapidly boil this. Cook for 10–12 minutes, stirring occasionally, until the liquid has been absorbed and the orzo is cooked.

6. Take it off the heat, then stir through the spinach, Parmesan and the lemon zest and juice. Taste for seasoning and adjust if needed. If it feels a little loose, leave it to stand for a minute or so, giving the orzo time to soak up the extra liquid, then serve.

Watt's the Story?

Orzo is becoming increasingly popular. If you've never heard of it, it's basically pasta that is shaped like rice. (It was named after the Italian word for barley, as it looks like a barley grain.) You can cook it in a similar way to risotto rice and, just like risotto, it's super-versatile and can be combined with all sorts of wonderful flavours. Even better, as it's a pasta, it cooks more quickly than rice.

Sausage & bean stew

• • • • • • • • • • • • • • • •

Try to find good butter beans for this recipe. If you can, pay a bit extra and get some really good-quality beans – such as a jar of Bold Bean Co 'queen' butter beans, which are seasoned and creamy in texture and, in my opinion, a game-changer brand – as they make such a difference. Dish this recipe up with a chunk of crusty bread and some peppery leaves.

serves: **2**
prep time: **10 mins**
cook time: **20 mins**

1 tablespoon olive oil
6 sausages, ideally higher-
   welfare
1 carrot, finely chopped
1 small onion, finely chopped
1 celery stick, finely chopped
2 garlic cloves, sliced
75ml white wine, chicken stock
   or water
400g can of butter beans (or
   see recipe introduction)
40g finely grated Parmesan
   cheese
2 tablespoons crème fraîche
finely grated zest and juice of
   1 lemon
salt and black pepper

1. Heat the oil in a pan over a medium-high heat. Cook the sausages until they are browned all over, then remove them from the pan, leaving the oil behind, and set aside.

2. Put the carrot in the same pan with the onion and celery. Cook for about 5 minutes, stirring occasionally, until they soften.

3. Add the garlic and cook for a further minute before pouring in the wine, stock or water and adding the beans along with the liquid from the can or jar.

4. Get the sausages back into the pan, bring the sauce to a simmer and cook for a few minutes.

5. Stir through the Parmesan, crème fraîche and lemon zest and juice. Taste for seasoning, adjust that if necessary, then serve.

One-pan beef & halloumi

· · · · · · · · · · · · · · · · ·

Vegetables, potato, minced beef and loads of cheese make up this delicious meal, perfect to place in the middle of the table, then dig in and share after a long day. It's lovely with some nice sourdough bread, or crunchy country bread, for dunking.

serves: **2**
prep time: **5 mins**
cook time: **20 mins**

1–2 tablespoons vegetable or
   sunflower oil
1 onion, finely chopped
1 carrot, finely chopped
1 celery stick, finely chopped
150g potatoes, chopped into
   1cm pieces
500g minced beef
4 garlic cloves, finely chopped
2 teaspoons dried oregano
400g can of chopped
   tomatoes
100g baby spinach
25g basil leaves
250g halloumi cheese, cut into
   1cm-thick slices
50g grated mozzarella cheese

1. Preheat the grill to high, or preheat the oven to 200°C fan.

2. Heat the oil in an ovenproof pan over a medium-high heat. Cook the onion, carrot, celery and potatoes for a few minutes, until they soften.

3. Add the minced beef and use a wooden spoon or spatula to gently break it up (try to avoid breaking up the potatoes, though), stirring and cooking until the meat is browned all over.

4. Chuck in the garlic and oregano and cook for a further minute before pouring in the tomatoes. Fill the empty can half-full with water and pour that in, too.

5. Bring the mixture to a simmer and cook for 15 minutes, or until the potatoes are tender.

6. Stir through the spinach and most of the basil, place the halloumi on top of the sauce, then sprinkle over the mozzarella.

7. Grill or bake until the cheese is golden, then scatter over the remaining basil leaves and take the sizzling pan to the table.

Mexican chicken traybake

• • • • • • • • • • • • • • • •

Black beans, lots of veggies and tender chicken thighs cooked with a Mexican spice mix, then served with a zesty green sauce. This may look like a long ingredients list, but in fact a lot of those items are spices, and, if you're starting to cook more often, you might well have begun to collect them in your spice rack.

serves: **4**
prep time: **10 mins**
cook time: **20 mins**

1 red pepper, sliced
1 yellow pepper, sliced
1 red onion, sliced
1 courgette, sliced into 5mm rounds
50g sliced jalapeños from a jar, drained
400g can of black beans, drained
6 tablespoons olive oil
finely grated zest and juice of 2 limes, plus lime wedges to serve
1 tablespoon ground cumin
1 tablespoon dried oregano
1 teaspoon chilli powder
1 teaspoon smoked paprika (not hot smoked)
½ teaspoon salt
½ teaspoon black pepper
8 boneless chicken thighs, with or without skin, as you prefer

For the sauce
100ml mayonnaise
50ml natural yogurt
finely grated zest and juice of 1 lime
20g coriander, chopped
50g spring onions, chopped
1 garlic clove, chopped

1. Preheat the oven to 200°C fan.

2. Place the red pepper, yellow pepper, red onion, courgette, jalapeños and black beans in a large roasting dish.

3. Spoon the olive oil into a bowl and add the lime zest and juice, the cumin, oregano, chilli powder, paprika, salt and pepper and mix everything well.

4. Pour half the spice mix into the veggies and stir to coat. Nestle the chicken thighs into the vegetables, then spoon the remaining spicy lime mixture over the chicken.

5. Bake for 20–25 minutes or until the chicken is cooked through. (If you cut into a larger piece of chicken, the juices should run clear. If not, continue to cook for another couple of minutes, then test again.)

6. Meanwhile, make the sauce by blending all the ingredients together with a stick blender until smooth.

7. Serve the chicken and veggies with the green sauce in a bowl on the side and lime wedges for squeezing over.

Watt's the Story?

This is one of those speedy midweek meals that can easily be tweaked if you are having friends over to eat. Just add hard shell or soft flour tortillas, tortilla chips, grated cheese (Wensleydale is good), sour cream and sliced avocado. If you also offer Little Gem lettuce leaves, it means that people who are gluten-free or intolerant can join in taco night too, using the leaves as wraps.

Jambalaya

• • • • • • • • • • • • • • • •

Coming to you from New Orleans, this is the ultimate one-pot meal of meat, prawns and vegetables with rice. It is easy to scale up and freezes well too, so it's worth making extra and sticking it in your freezer for another day.

serves: **4**
prep time: **5 mins**
cook time: **25 mins**

1–2 tablespoons vegetable or
   sunflower oil
1 onion, finely chopped
2 celery sticks, finely chopped
200g chorizo, chopped
5 garlic cloves, finely chopped
1 tablespoon Creole spice mix,
   or Cajun spice mix
1 red pepper, chopped
240g long grain rice
400g can of chopped
   tomatoes
500ml chicken stock
450g skinless boneless
   chicken thighs, cut into
   bite-sized pieces
180g raw shelled king prawns,
   halved lengthways
100g frozen peas
100g spring onions, sliced

1. Heat the oil in a large frying pan and fry the onion, celery and chorizo over a medium-high heat for a few minutes until the onion starts to soften.

2. Add the garlic and the spice mix and stir well, then tip in the red pepper and cook for 1 more minute.

3. Now add the rice, tomatoes, stock and chicken and again stir well.

4. Cover the pan with a lid or a sheet of foil and simmer over a medium-low heat for 20 minutes, or until the rice has cooked and most of the liquid has been absorbed.

5. For the last few minutes, add the prawns, peas and spring onions and stir well.

6. Once the prawns are cooked (they should be pink all over and will have firmed up) and all the liquid has been absorbed into the rice, the jambalaya is ready to serve.

Gone are the days when trying to copy your favourite takeaway food at home meant hours slaving away in the kitchen. In this chapter, I've put together a whole bunch of super-quick treat night meals, which prove you can save yourself a bit of money without any compromise on flavour.

Fast
Fakeaways

Firecracker salmon

● ● ● ● ● ● ● ● ● ● ● ● ● ● ● ●

So unbelievably easy, yet this delivers a real flavour explosion; I'm sure you'll love it. It was a really popular recipe online: people like how simple it is and it's ready in no time at all. It's definitely one of those dishes you cook when you want a treat, though it contains no oil at all. Dish it up with sticky rice and green vegetables (I like stir-fried Tenderstem broccoli and pak choi with this). You can also double the quantities to eat over the next few days.

serves: **4**
prep time: **5 mins**
cook time: **15 mins**

4 salmon fillets
4 tablespoons soy sauce
2 tablespoons soft brown sugar
2 tablespoons sriracha
juice of 2 limes
4 garlic cloves, finely chopped
   or grated
5g root ginger, finely chopped
   or grated
1 teaspoon chilli flakes
1 teaspoon paprika (not hot)
2 spring onions, sliced

1. Preheat the oven to 180°C fan.

2. Place the salmon skin side down in a baking dish.

3. Make the sauce. In a bowl, mix the soy sauce, sugar, sriracha, lime juice, garlic, ginger, chilli flakes and paprika. Pour it over the salmon to completely coat it.

4. Bake for 15 minutes, or until the salmon is cooked through.

5. Spoon the juices from the pan over the salmon, sprinkle over the spring onions and serve.

Garlic & paprika chicken

• • • • • • • • • • • • • • • • •

This was a viral sensation on social media in 2023. Maybe because it's ridiculously simple: just a handful of ingredients create the most delicious Eastern European-inspired dinner in a creamy sauce. Dish it up with Baby hasselbacks (see page 13) and seasonal veggies.

serves: **2**
prep time: **10 mins**
cook time: **15 mins**

50g plain flour
2 tablespoons paprika (not hot)
½ teaspoon salt
½ teaspoon black pepper
2 skinless chicken breasts
1 tablespoon vegetable or
 sunflower oil
4 garlic cloves, finely chopped
150ml chicken stock
150ml double cream
15g parsley leaves, chopped

1. Put the flour in a bowl with half the paprika, the salt and pepper. Mix well.

2. Slice the chicken breasts in half lengthways to give 4 thinner pieces. Coat each piece in the seasoned flour.

3. Heat the oil in a large frying pan, then cook the chicken over a medium-high heat until golden all over, 3–4 minutes on each side.

4. Remove the chicken from the pan, leaving the oil behind, then add the garlic and cook for 30 seconds, until aromatic. Pour in the stock and cream with the remaining paprika.

5. Get the chicken back into the pan, stir to coat, then bring to the boil and cook until the sauce is thick and creamy (3–4 minutes).

6. Sprinkle in the parsley and taste for seasoning, adjusting that if needed, then dish it up.

Pictured with Baby hasselbacks, see page 13.

Watt's the Story?

When a recipe asks for paprika, be careful to choose the right sort. For this dish, you need plain paprika, which gives a hint of spice but mostly just a great red pepper flavour. Definitely avoid jars labelled 'hot paprika', as that will make this dish overpoweringly hot. If you only have smoked paprika in, halve the quantity and use just 1 tablespoon in this recipe, or the smoky flavour will be too dominant.

Coconut prawn curry

• • • • • • • • • • • • • • • • •

A really great meal that combines both fresh and spicy flavours. Mango chutney is such an incredible ingredient to add to sauces and even to dressings – I sometimes use it in slaw – or, as here, in a curry, as it adds both tang and sweetness to a dish.

serves: **4**
prep time: **10 mins**
cook time: **10 mins**

For the spice paste
½ onion, chopped
2 garlic cloves
15g root ginger, peeled
2 teaspoons ground turmeric
2 teaspoons curry powder
1 red chilli, stalk removed,
   deseeded if you like less heat
10g coriander, stalks and
   leaves separated and
   chopped

For the curry
400ml can of coconut milk
1 tablespoon mango chutney
50g baby spinach
500g raw shelled king prawns
salt and black pepper
lime wedges, to serve

1. Put all the spice paste ingredients except for the coriander leaves in a blender, along with a splash of water. (The coriander stalks do go in the paste, so add them now if you haven't done so already.) Blend until smooth.

2. Scrape the spice paste into a pan and cook over a medium-high heat, stirring constantly, for a couple of minutes to release the flavours and aromas.

3. Pour in the coconut milk and add the mango chutney, then simmer for about 5 minutes until the sauce reduces slightly.

4. Add the spinach and prawns to the sauce and gently poach over a medium heat for 2–3 minutes, or until the prawns are cooked (they will be pink all over and will have firmed up).

5. Sprinkle in the coriander leaves, taste for seasoning and adjust it if needed, then serve the curry with a couple of lime wedges.

Thai green chicken curry

• • • • • • • • • • • • • • • • •

A lot of people love this dish but haven't made it from scratch, though my recipe means it's simple to get those authentic Thai flavours. With Thai green curry paste, you can bung it all in a blender and blitz it up for the most flavoursome mixture, and, when you smell the paste, it will change the game... all those fragrant spices and herbs make a heady mix. You'll be proud that you've made it yourself, and surprised at how simple it is, too. Serve this with jasmine or basmati rice, and maybe some prawn crackers if you want to push the boat out.

serves: **2–3**
prep time: **10 mins**
cook time: **15 mins**

For the curry paste
1 onion, finely chopped
2 tablespoons fish sauce
1 green chilli, or more if you like
  it hot, stalk removed, deseeded
  if you want less heat
1 lemongrass stalk, trimmed
  and chopped
1 teaspoon ground cumin
½ teaspoon ground coriander
2 garlic cloves, chopped
15g root ginger, chopped
finely grated zest and juice of
  1 lime, plus lime wedges to serve
25g bunch of coriander, stalks
  included
3 tablespoons vegetable or
  sunflower oil

For the rest
500g skinless boneless chicken
  thighs, cut into bite-sized pieces
400ml can of coconut milk
80g green beans
80g sugar snap peas, or
  mange tout
25g bunch of Thai basil leaves,
  chopped (optional)

1. Put all the ingredients for the curry paste, except for 1 tablespoon of oil, into a food processor and blitz until smooth.

2. Heat the remaining 1 tablespoon of oil in a large frying pan over a medium-high heat and cook the chicken until it's browned all over. Remove the chicken from the pan and set aside, then wipe out the pan with kitchen paper.

3. Add the curry paste to the dry pan and cook, stirring constantly, for a few minutes to release the flavours and aromas. Pour in the coconut milk and stir well.

4. Return the chicken to the pan, add the green beans and sugar snaps or mange tout and simmer for 5 minutes, until the chicken is cooked through and the sauce has thickened. (If you cut into a larger piece of chicken, the juices should run clear. If not, continue to cook for another couple of minutes, then test again.) Add a splash of water if the sauce gets too thick.

5. Scatter over the Thai basil leaves, if using, then serve with lime wedges, for squeezing.

Teriyaki salmon skewers

• • • • • • • • • • • • • • • • •

Here, you make a quick teriyaki sauce – one of those things, like sweet-and-sour sauce (see page 98) people think will be hard to make, but isn't – and smother the salmon with it to create this truly delicious Asian-inspired fish dish. It's worth making up a double recipe of teriyaki, then storing it for use in stir-fries. Covered and kept in the fridge, it is fine for a week or more. You can make this with chicken thighs, too, following the same method.

serves: **2**
prep time: **10 mins**
cook time: **15 mins**

For the teriyaki sauce
1 tablespoon cornflour
200ml water
5 tablespoons soy sauce
80g soft brown sugar
1 tablespoon mirin (or see
　page 120)
1 garlic clove, very finely
　chopped or finely grated
10g root ginger, finely grated

For the skewers
500g skinless salmon fillet
4 spring onions, each cut into 3,
　plus 2 more, sliced (optional),
　to serve
2 tablespoons vegetable or
　sunflower oil
1 teaspoon sesame seeds

1. Start by making the teriyaki sauce. Put the cornflour in a small bowl with the measured water and mix well. Pour it into a saucepan, then add the soy sauce, sugar, mirin, garlic and ginger.

2. Cook over a medium-high heat, stirring often, until the sauce thickens. Take it off the heat and leave to cool slightly.

3. Cut the salmon into bite-sized cubes and put it in a mixing bowl. Pour half the cooled teriyaki sauce over the fish and stir to coat.

4. Skewer a piece of salmon, followed by a piece of spring onion, alternating until you have 4 complete skewers (see photo, left).

5. Heat the oil in a large frying pan over a medium-high heat. Cook the salmon skewers for 4–5 minutes on each side, until cooked through. Brush over some of the remaining teriyaki sauce.

6. Finish by sprinkling over some sliced spring onions, if you like, and sesame seeds, then serve, with the remaining teriyaki sauce for dipping or drizzling.

Chicken rogan josh

• • • • • • • • • • • • • • • •

Rogan means 'red' in Hindi, and *josh* means 'passion', or, in this case, fiery or hot. Don't worry if you're not a chilli head though, as you can use a mild curry powder. Typically, this recipe is made with red meat such as mutton or lamb, but here I've used chicken to speed up the cooking.

serves: **2**
prep time: **10 mins**
cook time: **20 mins**

20g unsalted butter
1 teaspoon vegetable or
  sunflower oil
1 onion, finely chopped
1 cinnamon stick
2 cloves
2 garlic cloves, finely chopped
15g root ginger, finely chopped
  or finely grated
2 teaspoons paprika (not hot)
2 tablespoons hot curry
  powder (or mild, if you don't
  want it to be hot)
2 tablespoons tomato purée
400g can of chopped
  tomatoes
150ml chicken stock
400g skinless boneless chicken
  thighs, cut into bite-sized pieces
150g natural yogurt
10g coriander, chopped
salt and black pepper

1. Melt the butter with the oil over a medium-high heat. Add the onion, cinnamon stick and cloves and cook for about 5 minutes, or until the onion starts to turn golden.

2. Add the garlic and ginger and cook for another 30 seconds.

3. Stir in the paprika, curry powder and tomato purée and cook for a further minute.

4. Pour in the can of chopped tomatoes and the stock, then add the chicken and stir it well. Cover with a lid or a sheet of foil, bring it to a simmer and cook for about 15 minutes, or until the chicken is cooked through. (If you cut into a larger piece of chicken, the juices should run clear. If not, continue to cook for another couple of minutes, then test again.)

5. Stir in the yogurt and coriander, then taste for seasoning and adjust it if needed. Remove the cinnamon stick and any visible cloves. (Or, if you can't find them, just warn the people eating about them. They can be fished out and left on the side of the plate.)

6. Serve the rogan josh with rice and mango chutney, if you like.

Watt's the Story?

If you want to change things up, use a lamb shoulder in place of the chicken. Follow the recipe up until step 4, when the tomatoes and stock are added, then throw it in a slow cooker until the lamb is tender (about five hours on high). Stir in the yogurt and coriander when you come to dish it up.

Paneer tikka masala

Believe it or not, tikka masala is thought to have been created by British cooks from south Asia and it's often described as a British dish, despite now being popular all over the world. Usually it's cooked with chicken, but for this recipe I've used paneer. If you're not aware of paneer, you should get to know it! It's a mild-flavoured cheese with a nice texture that complements the curry sauce here perfectly. Great to eat on a cold night.

serves: **4**
prep time: **10 mins**
cook time: **20 mins**

4 tablespoons tikka spice mix, see below for homemade, or use shop-bought
400g paneer cheese
2 tablespoons natural yogurt
1–2 tablespoons vegetable or sunflower oil
1 onion, ideally red, finely chopped, plus more (optional) to serve
4 garlic cloves, finely chopped
15g root ginger, finely grated
1 tablespoon tomato purée
400g can of chopped tomatoes
150ml double cream
400g can of chickpeas, drained
2 tablespoons soft brown sugar
20g coriander, chopped
salt and black pepper

For the tikka spice
2 tablespoons garam masala
1 tablespoon ground cumin
1 tablespoon paprika (not hot)
1 teaspoon ground turmeric
1 teaspoon chilli powder

1. Mix together all the ingredients for the tikka spice, if you're making that from scratch.

2. Cut the paneer into 1cm chunks. Put it in a bowl with the yogurt and half the spice mix. Mix gently and leave to marinate while you get everything else ready.

3. Heat the oil in a large pan over a medium-high heat. Cook the onion for a few minutes until it starts to soften.

4. Chuck in the garlic, ginger, remaining spice mix and tomato purée. Cook for 2 more minutes.

5. Pour in the chopped tomatoes and cream, then add the chickpeas and marinated paneer, along with the marinade left in the bowl.

6. Bring to the boil, then reduce the heat and simmer the curry for 10 minutes. Stir through the sugar and chopped coriander, then taste for seasoning and adjust if needed. (You shouldn't need to add any salt, because of the paneer.)

7. Dish it up scattered with a few onion slivers, if you like, with basmati rice and naan.

Crispy sesame chicken

• • • • • • • • • • • • • • • • • •

I like this Asian crispy chicken dish with sticky rice, pak choi and lots of spring onions. For extra flavour, cook the chicken in sesame wok oil. Not to be confused with toasted sesame oil. You don't want to fry with toasted sesame oil, as the smoke point is very low and it will burn and give off toxins. Blended wok oil gets the flavour of sesame oil into a dish without any of those problems.

serves: **2**
prep time: **5 mins**
cook time: **15 mins**

400g skinless boneless
  chicken thighs
2 eggs, lightly beaten
50g plain flour
½ teaspoon salt
½ teaspoon black pepper
1 teaspoon paprika (not hot)
vegetable or sunflower oil, or
  sesame wok oil (see recipe
  introduction), to shallow-fry

For the sauce
4 tablespoons soy sauce
4 tablespoons tomato ketchup
2 tablespoons sriracha
2 tablespoons sweet chilli sauce
2 tablespoons toasted sesame oil
1 tablespoon mirin (or see page
  120)
25g soft brown sugar
4 garlic cloves, finely chopped
10g root ginger, finely chopped
  or finely grated

To serve (optional)
sesame seeds
sliced spring onions

1. Cut the chicken into bite-sized pieces.

2. Put the eggs in a bowl. Put the flour in another bowl with the salt, pepper and paprika and mix well.

3. Place the chicken pieces in the egg and coat completely, then dust each piece in the seasoned flour.

4. Heat a good amount of oil in a large frying pan, enough to lie about 2mm deep, then shallow-fry the chicken over a medium-high heat until it is golden brown and crispy. You may need to cook it in batches to avoid overcrowding in the pan. Once it is golden brown and crispy, remove from the pan and set aside on a sheet of kitchen paper, to blot off excess oil.

5. Put all the sauce ingredients in a clean pan and cook over a high heat for 2–3 minutes, until bubbling and sticky.

6. Add the chicken to the sauce and stir to coat. Cook for a couple of minutes over a medium heat.

7. Sprinkle with sesame seeds and sliced spring onions, if you like, then serve. This is great with steamed jasmine rice and pak choi.

Creamy Tuscan cod

• • • • • • • • • • • • • • • •

Just a handful of ingredients make up this creamy Italian-inspired sauce, with lightly poached cod fillets. This is pretty versatile; dish it up with rice, potatoes or even pasta. Cod is delicate and doesn't need loads of work: here, it just simmers in a sauce which carries so much flavour.

serves: **4**
prep time: **5 mins**
cook time: **15 mins**

4 skinless cod fillets
1–2 tablespoons olive oil
1 onion, finely chopped
4 garlic cloves, finely chopped
200ml vegetable stock
150ml double cream
80g baby spinach
2 tablespoons sundried
   tomato paste
40g finely grated Parmesan
   cheese
salt and black pepper

1. Season the cod with salt and pepper, then heat the oil in a large frying pan over a medium-high heat. Fry the cod for 2–3 minutes on each side, until it's almost cooked through.

2. Remove the fish from the pan, leaving the oil behind, and set aside. Add the onion to the pan and cook until it softens.

3. Chuck in the garlic and cook for a minute before pouring in the stock and cream.

4. Add the baby spinach and sundried tomato paste, stir well, then bring to a simmer.

5. Tip in the Parmesan and stir well, then get the cod fillets back in the pan. Cook until the sauce thickens (3–4 minutes), taste for seasoning and adjust that if necessary, then dish it up straight away.

Pictured with Lemony garlic greens, see page 19.

Ultimate honey-garlic chicken

I don't use the word 'ultimate' lightly, but this is so utterly delicious: crisp-coated chicken finished in a sweet, garlicky glaze. Every bite is so wonderfully flavourful. Serve it with rice and seasonal veggies.

serves: **2**
prep time: **10 mins**
cook time: **15 mins**

2 skinless chicken breasts
2 eggs, lightly beaten
60g plain flour
½ teaspoon salt
½ teaspoon black pepper
1 teaspoon paprika (not hot)
1 tablespoon vegetable or
  sunflower oil
25g unsalted butter, diced
6 garlic cloves, finely chopped
2 tablespoons cider vinegar
4 tablespoons soy sauce
100g honey
10g parsley leaves, finely
  chopped

1. Cut the chicken breasts in half lengthways to give 4 thinner pieces.

2. Put the eggs in a dish. In another, put the flour, salt, pepper and paprika, then mix it well.

3. Dip the chicken fillets in the egg, followed by the seasoned flour, to coat the pieces all over.

4. Heat the oil in a large frying pan and fry the chicken until it's golden and crispy on both sides and cooked through. (If you cut into a larger piece of chicken, the juices should run clear. If not, continue to cook for another couple of minutes, then test again.) Add the butter and, when it melts, chuck in the garlic. Cook for a minute.

5. Pour in the cider vinegar, soy sauce and honey, then cook until the sauce turns sticky and coats the chicken. If it gets too dry, stir a splash of water into the sauce.

6. Sprinkle in the parsley and stir it through, then serve.

Prawn & chorizo spaghetti

• • • • • • • • • • • • • • • • •

A simple pasta dish given piquancy with garlic, crème fraîche and lemon to cut through the richness of chorizo. Don't be afraid to add the Parmesan here: anyone claiming that cheese 'doesn't go' with seafood doesn't know what they're talking about! Trust me, try it out and see for yourself.

serves: **2**
prep time: **10 mins**
cook time: **15 mins**

200g spaghetti
1 tablespoon vegetable or
    sunflower oil
120g chorizo, cut into small
    chunks
150g raw shelled king prawns
4 garlic cloves, finely chopped
200ml crème fraîche
finely grated zest of 1 lemon
    (optional) and the juice of ½
50g finely grated Parmesan
    cheese, plus more to serve
10g parsley leaves, chopped
salt and black pepper

1. Drop the pasta into salted boiling water and cook according to the packet instructions. Drain, but reserve the pasta water.

2. Meanwhile, heat the oil in a large frying pan and cook the chorizo over a medium-high heat for a few minutes until it starts to turn crispy at the edges.

3. Add the prawns and the garlic and cook for another 2 minutes, stirring occasionally. The prawns should turn pink.

4. Use a ladle to add some of the pasta water to the pan, then add the crème fraîche, the lemon juice, Parmesan and parsley. Stir together.

5. Now add the drained pasta to the pan and toss to coat. If the sauce needs thickening, then stir it over the heat to reduce it a little. If it needs loosening up, add another ladle of pasta water.

6. Taste for seasoning, adjust that if needed, then finish with grated Parmesan and lemon zest, if you like.

Mongolian-style chicken

• • • • • • • • • • • • • • •

A twist on the popular Mongolian beef dish: delicious crispy chicken with a sweet and savoury sauce that can be ready in no time at all. Quick, simple and every bite packed full of flavour. Mongolia is a landlocked country between China and Russia, so this dish has Chinese influences, but not in the more familiar way. Give it a go; I'm sure you'll love it.

serves: **2**
prep time: **5 mins**
cook time: **15 mins**

450g skinless boneless
  chicken thighs
1½ tablespoons cornflour
2 tablespoons vegetable or
  sunflower oil
1 onion, sliced
100g spring onions, sliced, plus
  more to serve
4 garlic cloves, finely chopped
15g root ginger, finely chopped
1 red chilli, sliced
50ml chicken stock, or water
3 tablespoons soy sauce
2 tablespoons hoisin sauce
1 tablespoon toasted sesame oil
2 tablespoons soft brown sugar
sesame seeds, to serve

1. Cut the chicken into small bite-sized pieces. Pop it into a bowl, then add the cornflour and stir to coat.

2. Heat the oil in a large frying pan, or a wok. Cook the chicken over a medium-high heat until it's browned all over. This should take 5–6 minutes.

3. Add the onion and stir-fry for 1 minute. Then add the spring onions, garlic, ginger and chilli and stir-fry for 30 seconds more.

4. Pour in the stock or water, soy sauce, hoisin sauce and sesame oil, then add the sugar. Cook until the sauce becomes sticky.

5. Scatter over more spring onions and sesame seeds, then serve while it's all still piping hot.

Pork belly fried rice

Leftover cooked rice (or a store-bought pouch of microwave rice) is transformed into a glorious fast and flavourful dinner. Loaded with crispy pork belly, veggies and soy sauce, it is a real winner. Pork belly is popular because it's a juicy cut, but if you want leaner meat, you could substitute sliced pork loin instead. Great with a glass of beer at the end of a long day.

serves: **2**
prep time: **10 mins**
cook time: **20 mins**

200g pork belly slices, cut into small pieces
1–2 tablespoons vegetable or sunflower oil
1 onion, finely chopped
1 small carrot, finely chopped
¼ head of broccoli, chopped
220g cold cooked rice (or a shop-bought pouch)
60g frozen peas
2 tablespoons soy sauce
salt and black pepper

1. Season the pork belly with salt and pepper. Pour the oil into a wok or a large frying pan. Add the pork and cook over a high heat until it's golden and crispy.

2. Reduce the heat to medium-high, then add the onion, carrot and broccoli. Cook until the pork is cooked through and the vegetables are tender (3–4 minutes).

3. Add the rice, peas and soy sauce. Cook for 5–6 minutes, stirring occasionally, until it's thoroughly heated through, then taste for seasoning and adjust if needed, and serve.

Bang bang chicken

● ● ● ● ● ● ● ● ● ● ● ● ● ● ● ●

Sweet and spicy bang bang sauce is so incredibly tasty, and, with the tender chicken, it's the most amazing flavour explosion. This chicken is good over some sticky rice. Panko crumbs are a type of Japanese breadcrumbs that are large and flaky; they don't pack together when coating food, so stay crisper for longer.

serves: **4**
prep time: **5 mins**
cook time: **15 mins**

For the bang bang sauce
100ml sriracha
2 tablespoons sweet
  chilli sauce
1 tablespoon honey
100ml natural yogurt

For the chicken
60g plain flour
1 teaspoon paprika (not hot)
½ teaspoon salt
½ teaspoon black pepper
2 eggs, lightly beaten
150g panko crumbs (see recipe
  introduction), or regular dried
  breadcrumbs
2 large skinless chicken breasts
vegetable or sunflower oil, to
  shallow-fry

To serve (optional)
sesame seeds
sliced spring onions
finely sliced red chilli

1. Start by making the sauce: put all the ingredients into a bowl and mix well.

2. Get 3 separate dishes, in one put the flour, paprika, salt and pepper and mix well. Put the eggs in another, then tip the crumbs into the third bowl.

3. Cut the chicken breasts into bite-sized pieces, then coat the pieces in the seasoned flour, followed by the egg, then finally the crumbs.

4. Heat a good amount of oil in a large frying pan over a medium-high heat; you need enough oil to come halfway up the sides of the pieces of chicken. Once the oil is hot, shallow-fry the chicken pieces until they are golden and crisp all over. Once they are done, remove them from the pan and place on a plate lined with kitchen paper to blot off excess oil.

5. Serve the crispy chicken, drizzling over plenty of the bang bang sauce, then scatter with sesame seeds, spring onions and red chilli, if you like. Serve the remaining sauce on the side.

I have a very sweet tooth, so for me no meal is complete without a pudding, or any evening on the sofa without a biscuit. In this chapter, you will find some of my favourite sweet recipes that can be made quickly. From no-wait cheesecakes perfect for a dinner party dessert, to home-baked oatmeal-raisin cookies for snacking, or molten chocolate fondants to impress a date, I know you're going to love these.

Sweet
Treats

Chocolate orange cheesecakes

• • • • • • • • • • • • • • • • • •

This chocolate pud means a lot to me. It was the first recipe of mine that went viral, in fact it was pivotal for my career as it encouraged me to carry on sharing recipes with you. For the first time, people sent me photos of themselves making one of my recipes, which was a lovely feeling. It's also very festive and works well at Christmas time, but don't let that limit you!

serves: **6**
prep time: **25 mins**
cook time: **none**

For the base
200g chocolate bourbon biscuits
50g unsalted butter, melted

For the filling
135g dark Terry's chocolate
  orange, plus 6 segments
  to serve
100ml double cream
360g cream cheese
100g icing sugar
2 tablespoons cocoa powder
finely grated zest of 1 orange or
  mandarin (optional)

1. Place the bourbon biscuits in a sandwich bag, close the top, then use a rolling pin to smash them into crumbs. Pop the crushed biscuits into a bowl, pour in the melted butter and mix well.

2. Divide the buttery biscuit crumb between 6 glasses or ramekins. Press it down slightly, but not firmly.

3. Now for the filling. Melt the 135g chocolate orange in a microwave (see page 184 for tips), or in a heatproof bowl over a pan of simmering water (make sure the bowl does not touch the water). Set it aside for 10 minutes to cool slightly.

4. In a separate bowl, whip the double cream to stiff peaks.

5. In another large mixing bowl, mix the cream cheese, icing sugar and cocoa powder, then use an electric whisk to beat the mixture until smooth and thick.

6. Add the whipped cream and cooled melted chocolate orange and fold it through gently but thoroughly.

7. Divide the filling between the glasses or ramekins over the top of the buttery biscuit. Arrange segments of chocolate orange on top, then serve, scattered with orange or mandarin zest, if you like.

Oatmeal-raisin cookies

• • • • • • • • • • • • • • • •

Popular in the States, these are a lightly spiced and delicious alternative to a traditional chocolate cookie: save them for only those lucky people who deserve them. You can shape the dough into a log, freeze it, then slice off cookies to bake as and when you want. This recipe proved to be a favourite at the testing stage: a bunch of friends and followers baked these cookies and everyone loved them, so give them a go.

makes about **16**
prep time: **10 mins**
cook time: **10 mins**

120g unsalted butter, softened
120g granulated sugar
80g soft brown sugar
1 egg, lightly beaten
1 teaspoon vanilla bean paste
115g plain flour
½ teaspoon baking powder
½ teaspoon ground cinnamon
140g rolled oats
100g raisins

1. Preheat the oven to 190°C fan. Line 2 large baking trays with baking paper.

2. Put the softened butter in a large mixing bowl with the granulated sugar and soft brown sugar. Beat it all together until light and fluffy. Beat in the egg and vanilla.

3. Sift in the flour, baking powder and cinnamon, then fold it through until it's combined.

4. Add the oats and raisins and mix them in until all the ingredients are fully incorporated, but don't overwork the dough.

5. Use an ice-cream scoop to spoon the mixture on to the prepared trays, leaving 5cm between each cookie to allow for spreading.

6. Bake them for 10 minutes or until they are golden brown and slightly risen. Allow them to cool slightly before transferring to a wire rack to cool completely.

S'mores traybake

●●●●●●●●●●●●●●●●●

S'mores are popular in America: they are toasted marshmallows and chocolate sandwiched between digestive biscuits, traditionally toasted around a bonfire. This recipe involves chucking all the ingredients into a dish instead and baking it, then you take it to the table and all dig in together. It is fun to share: a real crowd-pleaser.

serves: **6**
prep time: **10 mins**
cook time: **10 mins**

10g unsalted butter
400g pink and white
  marshmallows
300g milk chocolate, broken
  into pieces, or milk chocolate
  chips, plus 100g more for
  the topping
225g digestive biscuits, broken
  into chunks
strawberries, to serve
  (optional)

1. Preheat the oven to 200°C fan. Lightly butter a baking dish with the butter.

2. Lay half the marshmallows in the dish, then top with half the chocolate and half the biscuits. Repeat with a second layer each of marshmallows, chocolate and biscuits.

3. Bake for about 10 minutes, until the marshmallows are golden and the chocolate has melted.

4. Meanwhile, melt the 100g chocolate for the topping either in a microwave (see below for tips) or in a heatproof bowl over a pan of simmering water, making sure the bowl does not touch the water.

5. Drizzle the s'mores with the melted chocolate and serve with strawberries, if you like, getting everyone to dig in with a spoon.

Watt's the Story?

Chocolate can 'seize' when you are trying to melt it, which means it clumps up and becomes sticky and lumpy. Unfortunately you can't save seized chocolate: nothing will make it smooth again. But you can avoid it seizing in the first place. (It will seize if it gets too hot, or comes into contact with water.) To melt chocolate in the microwave, break it up into a microwave-safe bowl and heat it in short bursts of 20–30 seconds, stirring in between each burst. Make sure to take the spoon out each time, especially if it's metal!

Cinnamon choux puffs

• • • • • • • • • • • • • • • • •

Inspired by Italian *zeppole*, these golden nuggets of fried choux pastry are tossed with caster sugar and ground cinnamon: they are delicious. You could serve them with custard, cream, ice cream or melted chocolate, so feel free to get creative. You can shape these by hand instead of with teaspoons, if you like, but if you do, you will need to oil your hands to stop the dough from sticking to them.

makes about **20**
prep time: **15 mins**
cook time: **10 mins**

60ml water
60ml milk
60g unsalted butter, diced
1 tablespoon caster sugar
65g plain flour
2 large eggs
vegetable or sunflower oil,
  to deep-fry

For the coating
1 tablespoon golden caster
  sugar
¼ teaspoon ground cinnamon

1. Put the measured water, milk, butter and sugar into a pan and bring it to the boil over a medium-high heat, stirring until the butter has melted and the sugar dissolved. Remove it from the heat and add the flour, beating with a wooden spoon until fully combined.

2. Place the pan back on the heat and cook for a further 2 minutes, stirring constantly, to remove any excess moisture.

3. Transfer the dough to a mixing bowl and use an electric whisk to beat for a minute to help it to cool down. Add the eggs, one at a time, beating well in between each addition until the dough is smooth and glossy.

4. Heat a good amount of oil in a large, deep pan: you want there to be at least 2cm depth of oil. If you have a thermometer, the oil should be at 180°C. If you don't have a thermometer, dip the handle of a wooden spoon into the oil: it should steadily start to bubble around the handle. Meanwhile, mix the sugar and cinnamon for coating in a small bowl.

5. Use 2 teaspoons to scoop out the dough, then spoon a batch of about 5 mini puffs into the hot oil and fry for 4–5 minutes, making sure to turn them over halfway if they don't turn on their own. The pan should not be overcrowded and these will expand once they hit the hot oil, so don't try to cook too many at once.

6. Once they are done, transfer them with a slotted spoon to a plate lined with kitchen paper to blot off the excess oil. Repeat to cook the remaining puffs in the oil, adjusting the heat under the pan as necessary.

7. When they are all done, put them in a mixing bowl and toss together with the sugar and cinnamon to coat, then serve straight away, or as soon as possible.

Chocolate mousse

• • • • • • • • • • • • • • • • • •

This gorgeous, rich dessert is filled with bonus white chocolate chips and chunks of digestive biscuit, to give both crunch and extra deliciousness. It is made with cream, which helps to thicken the mousse, so it's ready to eat as soon as it is made, if you like; otherwise this will keep in the fridge for up to three days. Don't worry about the recipe containing raw egg whites: in the United Kingdom, eggs which have the Red Lion stamp are deemed safe to eat raw, as the hens have been vaccinated against salmonella.

serves: **6**
prep time: **20 mins**
cook time: **none**

200g milk chocolate, broken
  into pieces
200ml double cream
4 egg whites (you can use the
  yolks in Meatball carbonara,
  Chocolate chip shortbread or
  Molten chocolate fondants,
  see pages 63, 190 and 196)
60g digestive biscuits, broken
  into small pieces
60g white chocolate chips
salt

For the topping
100ml double cream
2 teaspoons vanilla bean paste
20g milk chocolate, finely
  chopped, or shaved with
  a vegetable peeler

1. Melt the chocolate either in a microwave (see page 184 for tips) or in a heatproof bowl over a pan of simmering water, making sure the bowl does not touch the water. Once melted, set aside to cool for 10 minutes.

2. Pour the cream into a bowl and whip to soft peaks.

3. Put the egg whites in another bowl with a pinch of salt and whisk until they reach stiff peaks.

4. Fold the cooled melted chocolate into the cream, then gently fold through the egg whites with a spatula.

5. Carefully fold through the biscuit pieces and white chocolate chips, then divide the mixture between 6 espresso cups, glasses or ramekins.

6. For the topping, put the cream and vanilla into a bowl and whip to soft peaks. Spoon it over the mousse, then sprinkle over the chopped or shaved chocolate.

7. You can enjoy these right away for a softer mousse, or pop them in the fridge to chill, where they will firm up.

Chocolate chip shortbread

• • • • • • • • • • • • • • • •

Packed full of chocolate chips, these are are truly delicious and perfect for sharing, or just for enjoying on your own with a cup of tea.

makes about **12**
prep time: **5 mins**
cook time: **20 mins**

340g plain flour, plus more to dust
220g unsalted butter, diced
100g golden caster sugar, plus
　more to sprinkle
150g chocolate chips, milk or
　dark, as you prefer
2 egg yolks

1. Preheat the oven to 170°C fan. Line a large baking tray with baking paper.

2. Tip the flour into a large mixing bowl, then add the butter. Rub the flour and butter between your fingers until the mixture looks like even crumbs.

3. Add the sugar and the chocolate chips and mix them in. Now add the egg yolks, then squish everything together to form a dough. Do this as quickly as possible, as you don't want to overwork the dough.

4. Once it has all come together, roll it out on a floured surface to about 1cm thick, then it cut into rounds using a 7cm biscuit cutter.

5. Transfer the shortbreads on to the prepared tray, spacing them evenly apart, and sprinkle with a little more caster sugar.

6. Bake in the oven for 20 minutes or until they are lightly golden. Leave the biscuits to cool for 5 minutes on the tray before carefully transferring to a wire rack to cool completely.

7. As soon as they are cool, they are ready to eat!

Watt's the Story?

Technically, shortbread is just sugar, butter and flour, but using egg yolks here creates a texture somewhere between biscuit and shortbread. That makes this recipe more foolproof, as the egg helps to bind the biscuit dough and keep it together, yet the biscuits retain that classic shortbread feel: people eating these wouldn't know unless you told them.

No-wait strawberry cheesecake

A great-looking pudding, ready in 25 minutes, which you can serve immediately to a table of people who, I promise, will be blown away. When I was first thinking about this recipe, I was imagining someone making it on the day of a dinner party, as it's a classic but is no faff at all. You can substitute the strawberries with blueberries or raspberries, if you prefer.

serves: **6**
prep time: **25 mins**
cook time: **none**

For the topping
200g strawberries, hulled
  and chopped
2 tablespoons icing sugar
juice of ½ lemon
mint leaves (optional)

For the base
90g digestive biscuits
25g unsalted butter, melted

For the filling
100g white chocolate
100ml double cream
360g cream cheese
100g icing sugar
1 teaspoon vanilla bean paste
200g strawberries, hulled
  and chopped

1. Start by preparing the topping, to give the strawberries a chance to macerate. Put the strawberries in a bowl with the icing sugar and lemon juice. Mix well, then set aside.

2. Now for the base. Place the biscuits in a sandwich bag, close the top, then use a rolling pin to smash them into crumbs. Pop the crushed biscuits into a bowl, pour in the melted butter and mix well. Spoon the buttery biscuit crumb between 6 glasses or ramekins. Press it down slightly, but not firmly.

3. To make the filling, melt the white chocolate either in a microwave (see page 184 for tips), or in a heatproof bowl over a pan of simmering water (making sure the bowl does not touch the water). Be aware that white chocolate melts a lot more quickly than milk chocolate, so be careful not to burn it. Leave to cool slightly.

4. In a separate bowl, whip the double cream to stiff peaks.

5. Put the cream cheese in another large mixing bowl with the icing sugar, vanilla and cooled melted white chocolate. Use an electric whisk to beat until smooth and thick.

6. Add the whipped cream and chopped strawberries for the filling to the cream cheese mixture and gently but thoroughly fold them evenly through.

7. Divide the filling between the 6 glasses or ramekins over the buttery biscuit bases. Spoon the macerated strawberries on top. Scatter with mint leaves, if you want, and serve straight away.

Zesty tiramisu

● ● ● ● ● ● ● ● ● ● ● ● ● ● ● ● ●

The ultimate Italian trifle with a twist. Even though I'm not a fan of coffee, I LOVE this tiramisu: the orange and lemon freshen and complement it so well. It is a simplified version – as are many of my recipes – because the sometimes-tricky traditional Italian cream filling has been substituted by my very stable adaptation. This means that even novice cooks don't have anything to worry about here.

serves: **8**
prep time: **30 mins**
cook time: **none**

For the coffee soak
3 tablespoons instant coffee
   granules
2 tablespoons golden caster sugar
300ml boiling water
4 tablespoons Kahlua, or other
   coffee liqueur (optional)

For the tiramisu
500g mascarpone, or cream
   cheese
300ml double cream
120g golden caster sugar
finely grated zest and juice of
   2 oranges, plus more zest
   to serve
finely grated zest and juice of
   2 lemons
300g sponge fingers
2 tablespoons cocoa powder

1. Prepare the coffee soak. Put the coffee granules and sugar into a jug or a bowl. Pour in the measured boiling water and stir until the coffee and sugar dissolve, then set aside to cool down. Once it's cool, pour the coffee liqueur in, if using, then mix.

2. Put the mascarpone or cream cheese in a large mixing bowl with the cream, sugar and the orange and lemon zest and juice. Use a whisk to beat until smooth. Use a tablespoon to take out 8 spoons of the cream and set aside, to serve with the finished dish.

3. Get a large dish, measuring about 30 × 20cm. Dip half the sponge fingers one at a time in the coffee soak for about 5 seconds, arranging them in the dish in a single layer as they are done.

4. Spoon in half the mascarpone cream and spread it evenly over the sponge fingers.

5. Now repeat with another layer of coffee-soaked sponge fingers, followed by the remaining mascarpone cream.

6. Cover the tiramisu and put it in the fridge until you are ready to serve. Before serving, dust the cocoa powder liberally all over.

7. Grate some orange zest over the tiramisu, then serve it with a bowl of the reserved cream on the side.

Molten chocolate fondants

• • • • • • • • • • • • • • • • •

This is usually a recipe for the more advanced baker, but, following my simple steps, it's achievable for anyone. It's the ultimate dinner party dessert, as I've also added a method for a quick and easy caramel sauce to go with it. Serve this with ice cream or crème fraîche. You will need pudding moulds for this; you can easily buy reasonably priced foil moulds online.

You can make the fondants up to three days ahead and store them in the fridge: just add a minute or two on to the baking time if you're planning to cook them straight from the fridge.

serves: **4**
prep time: **15 mins**
cook time: **8 mins**

For the fondants
120g unsalted butter
cocoa powder, to dust
100g dark chocolate,
  70% cocoa solids, broken
  into pieces
2 large eggs, plus 1 egg yolk
100g golden caster sugar
100g plain flour

For the caramel sauce
150g caster sugar
4 tablespoons water
50g unsalted butter, chopped
100ml double cream

To serve (optional)
ice cream, or crème fraîche
toasted chopped hazelnuts

1. Preheat the oven to 200°C fan. Get 4 moulds ready: use 20g of the butter and divide it between the moulds, rubbing it all over their insides and making sure there are no dry gaps. Then dust the moulds with cocoa powder so that each has a nice coating. Place the moulds in the fridge while you get the chocolate mix ready.

2. Dice the remaining butter. Melt the chocolate and butter in a heatproof bowl over a pan of simmering water, making sure the bowl does not touch the water. When it's completely melted, take it off the heat and set aside to cool slightly.

3. Put the eggs and egg yolk in a mixing bowl with the sugar and whisk with electric beaters until pale and thick. Sift in the flour and gently fold it all together.

4. Pour the cooled melted chocolate into the mix and beat together; it will shrink slightly and should resemble a loose cake batter. Tip the mix into a jug, then pour it into the prepared moulds, filling each of them about two-thirds of the way up.

5. Bake them for 8 minutes, then leave them to stand for at least 2 minutes before turning them out. If you have left them to stand and coated the moulds well, they should just slide out with no fuss.

6. Meanwhile, make the caramel sauce. Tip the sugar into a heavy-based pan along with the measured water. Cook over a medium heat until you have a caramel: the sugar should be golden, but not burnt. Take off the heat and beat in the butter and then the cream. Leave to cool slightly before serving.

7. Serve the fondants with the slightly cooled caramel sauce, with ice cream or crème fraîche and toasted hazelnuts, if you like.

Thank you!!

I'll tell you something: it's been one hell of a journey to get to this point, but I'm so proud that I'm here, living in this moment and able to share this book with you.

Many years ago, when I first googled 'how to publish a cookbook', the thing I read time and again was that I should 'grow a big social following'. It's definitely not an easy task, but through dedication, hard work and – probably most importantly – consistency, I have managed to grow a social audience of well over a million people.

Whether you've been there from the beginning, found me more recently, or even discovered me through this book, you're the reason I'm able to share my passion in this way with so many people and I don't take you for granted. So thank **YOU**.

On to the book people. Rowan Yapp, thank you for sliding in to my DMs, believing in the dream, then guiding me through publishing this book. To Lena Hall, Shunayna Vaghela, Isobel Turton and the team at Bloomsbury: you have been an absolute dream to work with, with your bubbly characters and passion. I appreciate you all so much.

Now for the creative team – also known as 'the dream team' – who helped to bring this book to life. Behind the incredible photography was the amazing Jonathan Gregson, a giant in the food photography world and I can see why. Max Barstow, Jonathan's assistant who is also a human encyclopaedia, injecting interesting facts to all our on-shoot conversations.

Heading up the kitchen was food stylist Valerie Berry. Before I'd met Valerie, everyone had spoken so highly of her and it was an absolute pleasure to learn why. She is the most humble person I have ever met, quietly but confidently proving her reputation. Assisting in the kitchen were Alice Earll and Eden Owen-Jones who, as well as preparing food, filled the shoot days with character. Sorting out all the props was Tab Hawkins. As well as having a great eye for what will look good for each dish, she was also a ray of sunshine who could often be found dancing around the studio. And a big thank you to Aya and Georgia for coming on board for the final shoot day.

Working behind the scenes designing every part of this book was Anna Green. When I saw the chapter designs for the first time, I realised Anna's vision for this book was exactly what I had wanted it to be. I'm sure you'll agree this book is looking so incredible.

Writing a book is a hard thing for anyone to do and involves a lot of words! That's where Lucy Bannell comes in, taking my words and elevating them to sound much better and easier to read. Lucy has made subtle changes and suggestions that have taken this book to the next level.

So, to the creative dream team, **THANK YOU**, I appreciate you. This book is as much yours as it is mine.

Now on to the more personal thank yous. As I said at the start, it's been one hell of a journey and there have been so many people who helped me along the way. It would be impossible to include everyone, but I'll give it a go.

To my family who have stuck by me throughout everything, even when things were real bad. Mum, Paul, Dad, David, Lauren, Hayley, Alex, and of course my number one fan Amy. I can't leave out my cousin James either, with many midnight phone calls over the years often encouraging me and pushing me to achieve more.

I also need to thank my clients who I cook for. As I write this, I have two regular clients who are incredibly supportive of what I do. They are flexible, so that I can work around the sometimes hectic life that I lead, they offer stability financially, but also stability in giving me routine and regular human interaction. This fun journey I'm on would be a lot more difficult without you.

There have been many chefs that have helped me along the way, but one, Ian Nagelson, needs mentioning. This is the guy who came into the prison and offered me a job. It was more than a job though, it was a lifeline. My life would look very different had I not met Ian. He didn't just give me a job, he nurtured me and taught me discipline. I've told the story before about how he had me iron my chef whites and be in the kitchen an hour before anyone else, teaching me a great work ethic that continues to this day.

And finally, thank you to the staff at Reading prison between 2008 and 2011 who played a part in helping me become the person I am today. Over the last decade, I've been into prisons and seen the work that some of the staff do, and nine times out of ten they are going above and beyond what their job role encompasses. Chris Simmons (Simmo) and David Stretton (Stretts) are two examples of this, with everything they did to ensure young people, including me, were able not only to complete the Duke of Edinburgh award, but also to excel.

For anyone else who thinks they deserve a thank you, you probably do, so thank you too.

Index

About the author

Jon Watts is a professional chef, recipe creator and influential social media chef.

After getting into serious trouble as a teenager, Jon was sentenced to six and a half years in a young offenders' institute. He was determined not to fall into the vicious cycle of reoffending, so he took on every opportunity he could to learn and develop. One of those opportunities was working towards Duke of Edinburgh awards. As part of this he had to pick a skill to learn and he picked cooking. He was the first person in custody to achieve all three Bronze, Silver and Gold DofE awards.

Jon secured a job in one of Jamie Oliver's restaurants, where he worked for several years before setting up on his own. As well as starting up his own food truck business, Jon quickly became a sought-after corporate and events chef, cooking for many well-known people and businesses, including regularly catering at Windsor Castle.

Jon gained national exposure through his social media profile and TV appearances, including cooking live on ITV's *This Morning* multiple times. His recipes have gained a reputation for being simple yet delicious and always using ingredients that are easily accessible and budget friendly.

In 2023 he self-published his first cookbook, *Watts Cooking*, which was a huge success.

Away from cooking, Jon tells his story to many different audiences, from motivational speeches for businesses, to talking in prisons and schools to at-risk young people.

BLOOMSBURY PUBLISHING
Bloomsbury Publishing Plc
50 Bedford Square, London, WC1B 3DP, UK
29 Earlsfort Terrace, Dublin 2, Ireland

BLOOMSBURY, BLOOMSBURY PUBLISHING
and the Diana logo are trademarks of Bloomsbury Publishing Plc

First published in Great Britain in 2024
Text © Jon Watts, 2024

Photographs © Jonathan Gregson, 2024

Jon Watts and Jonathan Gregson have asserted their right under the Copyright, Designs and
Patents Act, 1988, to be identified as Author and Photographer, respectively, of this work.

For legal purposes, the acknowledgements on pages 198–199 constitute an extension of
this copyright page.

A catalogue record for this book is available from the British Library.
ISBN: HB: 978-1-5266-7745-7; eBook: 978-1-5266-7743-3;
2 4 6 8 10 9 7 5 3 1

Project Editor: Lucy Bannell
Designer: Anna Green
Photographer: Jonathan Gregson
Food Stylists: Valerie Berry and Aya Nishimura
Prop Stylist: Tabitha Hawkins
Indexer: Vanessa Bird
Printed and bound in China by C&C Offset Printing Co.,Ltd

To find out more about our authors and books,
visit www.bloomsbury.com and sign up for our newsletters.